Learning and Assessing with Multiple-Choice Questions in College Classrooms

Multiple-choi...   ...d in college
classrooms, ye...   ...to maximize
the questions'...   ...ce *Questions*
in College Cl...   ...l to enable
instructors an...   ...ugh the use
of MCQs. Inc...   ...:, leveraging
technology, ar...   ...ncrease the
benefits of a c...   ...earning and
assessment to...   ...ove student
outcomes.

Jay Parkes i...   ... College of
Education at t...

Dawn Zimma... ...   ...at the Open
Learning Initi...

D0303246

38783A

Learning and Assessing with Multiple-Choice Questions in College Classrooms

Jay Parkes and
Dawn Zimmaro

Routledge
Taylor & Francis Group

NEW YORK AND LONDON

First published 2016
by Routledge
711 Third Avenue, New York, NY 10017

and by Routledge
2 Park Square, Milton Park, Abingdon, Oxon, OX14 4RN

Routledge is an imprint of the Taylor & Francis Group, an informa business

Library of Congress Cataloging in Publication Data
Names: Parkes, Jay. | Zimmaro, Dawn.
Title: Learning and assessing with multiple choice questions in college classrooms / Jay Parkes and Dawn Zimmaro.
Description: New York : Routledge, 2016. | Includes bibliographical references.
Identifiers: LCCN 2015037841 | ISBN 9781138845978 (hardback) | ISBN 9781138845985 (pbk.) | ISBN 9781315727769 (e-book)
Subjects: LCSH: Multiple-choice examinations. | Educational tests and measurements. | Education, Higher.
Classification: LCC LB3060.32.M85 P37 2016 | DDC 371.26–dc23
LC record available at http://lccn.loc.gov/2015037841

ISBN: 978-1-138-84597-8 (hbk)
ISBN: 978-1-138-84598-5 (pbk)
ISBN: 978-1-315-72776-9 (ebk)

Typeset in Goudy
by Cenveo Publisher Services

Contents

Figures

Tables

Preface

Whether in the chilled, wind-whipped snow squalls of February or the dappled sunshine of August, we frequently stepped out onto the second-story balcony of the Schreyer Institute for Innovation in Learning at Penn State to catch some fresh air and to take a break from our assessment consulting duties. That balcony heard a great many conversations among all of the folks who worked there about assessment, instructional design and the challenges of working with faculty who wanted to improve their teaching.

We were both earning our PhDs in Educational Psychology with emphases in Applied Measurement at Penn State. We both were advisees of Hoi Suen, now Distinguished Professor of Educational Psychology at Penn State. We each learned an incalculable amount from Dr. Suen through those formal and informal ways one learns from one's dissertation advisor. We still hear his advice ringing in our ears. Jay hears Dr. Suen's voice sometimes when Jay is talking to his own advisees. Dawn often recalls Dr. Suen's sage advice to "have a conversation with your audience about what you know" when giving an assessment talk or workshop. No doubt, were Dr. Suen to read this book, he would find numerous ideas which are his. We mean those as flattery, not theft. This book definitely began with him.

We had both been employed as Assessment Consultants at the Schreyer Institute. We worked around lots of faculty members who wanted to make changes in student learning and in their own teaching, and had sought out the consulting at the Schreyer Institute. We learned a great deal from them about the courage it took to make such changes, and we grew to respect them and that courage. Since you've picked up this book, we suspect you're pretty courageous, too, to consider multiple-choice as a vehicle for learning. It's not entirely inaccurate to say this book has roots on that Schreyer Institute balcony.

In 1998, Jay graduated and took his first, and so far only, academic position as a member of the Educational Psychology faculty at the University of New Mexico. In the years since, he has taught courses in classroom assessment, educational measurement, research design, and educational statistics. And he's done lots of workshops on multiple-choice testing. His research has largely revolved around the theme of treating assessments as cognitive events. That is, rather than thinking about tests and other assessments as static probes, what possibilities emerge if they are viewed as thought processes? This book grows up out of that work, too.

Dawn finished her degree in 2003 and continued her journey as an assessment and measurement consultant at the University of Texas at Austin, eventually becoming the Director of Assessment for UT's Center for Teaching and Learning. She collaborated with faculty and administrators to research and evaluate classroom redesigns and instructional innovations. Along the way she has taught many workshops for faculty and graduate students on a myriad of assessment issues, with writing multiple-choice questions being one of the most requested topics. More recently, Dawn's work at the Open Learning Initiative at Stanford University has focused on developing assessments and learning analytics for online learning systems. She also has had the opportunity to teach an undergraduate statistics class and graduate class in educational and psychological testing to better understand some of the challenges that go along with being in the classroom. Since her time at Penn State, Dawn's work has revolved around collaborating with instructors to develop fair and reliable classroom and online assessments that measure the type of learning in which they want their students to engage. This book is influenced by the thoughtful and challenging questions she has received from instructors throughout the years.

We jointly wish to dedicate this book to Hoi Suen, Distinguished Professor of Educational Psychology at Penn State, for getting us started down our professional paths. He is definitely in this book. Jay would like to dedicate this book to Morag Smith and William and Sarah, the best of choices! Dawn would like to dedicate this book to Wills, Logan, and Evan, the key to her success!

Jay Parkes
University of New Mexico

Dawn Zimmaro
Stanford University

September 2015

1 Introduction

So you're using multiple-choice questions. That's wonderful! Multiple-choice questions are one of the most researched and widespread educational measurement tools in existence. They have many, many advantages, as we'll discuss. Maybe you already know that. Lots of faculty members choose multiple-choice for their classes because they permit broad content coverage in a short period of time; they're easy and quick to score, which facilitates feedback to students; they can be administered easily through technological means. Actually the list of advantages is pretty long, and we'll discuss most of those items in depth throughout this book.

We want to acknowledge, though, that maybe you've selected multiple-choice questions but you're not happy or enthusiastic about it. You sound resigned. You sound like this is a corner you've been backed in to. You'd rather be using essay tests, or projects, or presentations, or papers or electronic portfolios to assess your students, but your classes are just too big. Maybe the licensing or credentialing exam in your field uses multiple-choice so you feel you need to also so your students are ready for that exam. Perhaps because of accreditation or institutional accountability pressures, your students need to participate in course-wide or program-wide tests which are not of your own choosing.

You've never really been enamored of multiple-choice questions (MCQs). Students need only recognize and not recall or construct the right answer. They can guess the right answer. Perhaps you think multiple-choice can only address lower-level thinking. And now you've got security issues with copies of previous semesters' tests out there. And now it's easier for your students to cheat on your exams.

You sound just like some colleagues of ours, or at least like these composite avatars of colleagues of ours. Do any of these faculty members' situations sound familiar to you?

Olivia Peña has just been tenured and promoted to Associate Professor of History at a large suburban community college in the Western US, and her department chair has asked her to teach the large section of the general education required US History to 1877 with about 300 students in it.

The others who have taught the course have used multiple-choice tests, of course, but one of the reasons the chair would like Olivia to move into the course is that some changes are afoot, and he'd like fresh (and frankly, younger) eyes to have a look at it. Two major changes have occurred. First, the college is coming up on its Accrediting Commission for Community and Junior Colleges reaccreditation visit in a couple of years and the Dean has been preaching outcomes assessment really hard. Second, the Chair has noticed an uptick in cheating allegations coming out of that course. So things need to change and Dr. Peña is just the one to get them done!

Professor Preet Shah, a psychology professor, teaches at a mid-sized, four-year university located in the Midwest. Her university has a well-known distance education program that attracts learners from across the world. Her department chair has asked her to develop a fully online introductory statistics course that is applicable for both psychology majors and non-majors and will be offered for college credit. Dr. Shah previously taught this course as a face-to-face course with an enrollment of approximately 75 students.

After consulting with the distance education office at her institution, she learns that the learners who enroll in her course will include students at her university seeking an online alternative to the face-to-face version, college students working toward a degree at another institution, individuals seeking professional enrichment, and high school students pursuing dual credit. The distance education office informs her that she can expect between 800 and 1,000 students enrolled in the class for a given semester.

Professor Shah is a bit overwhelmed at the thought of teaching almost 1,000 students with such varying backgrounds and reasons for enrolling in her class. She previously has used MCQs for her in-class quizzes and has some questions on her classroom exams. She realizes that given the fully online delivery format and the number of students this course will now serve, she will need to expand her use of MCQs in her assessments.

It's only been a couple of years since Sam Oliver was promoted to full Professor of Biology at a mid-size East Coast public doctoral level university. With that milestone behind him, he relaxed a bit, took a look around, and rediscovered his deep joy in teaching. One of his favorites is a junior-level course for majors, one of the first where they truly begin to specialize. This transition comes with an increased reading load for the students as well as higher expectations for reading critically and synthesizing those readings. As part of his recommitment to teaching, he took a workshop about writing across the curriculum, and he really liked the idea of a reading journal. With the increased expectations of students regarding reading, this seemed like a great way not only to encourage them to read the assignments before class but also to drive some of the critical reading and thinking. He's actually found he enjoyed reading and responding to the journals, which surprised him a bit.

He's been teaching one of several sections with about 20 students although the recent recession and attendant budget cut-backs at the university have driven the consolidation of those sections. So now he'll be teaching about 50 students in a section. With that many students and without the support of any teaching assistants, he simply will not be able to retain the reading journals. He's done some talking around campus to some of his other colleagues in the natural sciences and to the director of the university's Center for Excellence in Teaching. He's always been reluctant to use multiple-choice questions for lots of reasons but perhaps some weekly quizzes could meet some of the goals that the reading journals were meeting.

You might notice some similarities. None of these three initially chose MCQs but circumstances have led them to that choice. All of them actually have some pretty valid and compelling reasons to use MCQs. Perhaps you are in a similar situation.

Take heart! All is not lost! One of the central premises of this book is that "Assessments don't hurt students; people with assessments hurt students." You and Olivia and Preet and Sam don't have to be one of those people. You're looking glum about having decided to use MCQs because you think the die is cast. Far from it! The decision to use MCQs was the first of many you and Sam will make (or that will be made for you through default and neglect) that will determine what exactly your exams will measure and whether they benefit your students or do them some harm. You and Sam have not yet completely determined that you'll never see critical thinking on exams. Whether your students are robbed of significant learning experiences because you have chosen to use multiple-choice questions *yet depends* on what you and they do before, during, and after they take the exam. You and Preet can conclude that teaching completely online to a large number of students resigns you to giving up on using assessments as learning tools or that you might be able to leverage technology in new ways to support how your students learn from their assessments. You and Olivia yet have the choice before you to administer a sterile measurement probe of learning objectives from which you and they will learn little and will be baffled by, or to engage in a layered set of learning experiences with your students as you and they together prepare for, take, and learn afterward from a multiple-choice test. This book will explore many different strategies to do this.

We don't really mean to deepen your gloom, but were those papers and essay tests really that great? Take a moment to reflect: Have you gotten deep, engaged critical thinking on those essay tests, papers, or projects? Have you ever sat slumped over a set of papers and sighed, "They didn't get it!"? How often have their essay responses been regurgitated textbook language, sometimes to the point of plagiarism? Olivia has seen a lot of that. Sam is very familiar with that frustration and nausea when he realized the trash can at the end of the hallway outside his office contained half of his class's papers full of his copious, insightful comments about how to improve their work? Did those students get any more use out of those comments than they would have gotten from a "72 percent" that they read off a sheet taped to his office door? *It's what you and your students do before the assessment (regardless of format), what happens during that assessment, and what you and your students do afterwards, that steer the benefits of assessments for students.* Preet's experiences in her face-to-face course with MCQs leads her to believe that the assessment format itself does not determine the kind of thinking students do on assessments; the format is, at best, an invitation to certain kinds of thinking. That's another central tenet of this book.

Be honest; you've not been totally unhappy about this choice. Part of you is looking forward to the relative ease and speed of using multiple-choice questions. Preet is intrigued by all of the automated assessment and grade-book functions that her university's course management system provides. No more waiting 48 hours for bubble sheets to be scanned! Olivia thinks taking questions out of a textbook item bank and letting a computer do the scoring of the bubble sheets has *got* to be easier than grading a stack of papers. She's right – sort of. Good assessment is hard work for you and for the students regardless of what the assessment format is. Your choice of assessment format (e.g. MCQs versus essay test) is, at best, a choice of where in the process you will spend your energy. In an essay test, Preet typically spends more time scoring responses than she does writing questions, while in a multiple-choice test, she typically spends more time writing questions than she does scoring them. But significant planning, thought, and work goes in to either. You haven't truly made a choice about the time and energy you'll spend assessing your students by choosing MCQs.

So take heart! You and Sam and Preet and Olivia have many, many choices yet to make which will determine how well MCQs work for you and your students. And the core tenet of this book is: MCQs *and how you and your students use them* can work extraordinarily well for you both.

Why Students Hate Tests, But They Won't Hate Yours

While we're being honest, there are endless reasons why students hate tests. We would wager, though, that the truth is that students hate *poor* tests. We will draw on bodies of research and vast stores of experience when differentiating good, or better, tests from bad, or poor ones. And, given our maxim that "Assessments don't hurt students; people with assessments hurt students," students don't much like *uninformed* or perhaps even *unscrupulous* test-givers. There are unscrupulous test-givers out there; instructors who play tricks on students and may even be dishonest. We will address unscrupulous test-giving. Much, much more common is what, for ease of reference, we'll refer to as the "uninformed test-giver". Teaching and assessing students draw on your own values and philosophies as a person and as an educator, and yet, among the professorate, test-givers with explicit values and philosophies which they can articulate for themselves, their students, and anyone else who asks are rare. In the absence of such explicit, articulate, systematic principles, we tend to make ad hoc decisions about assessment, ones which change from student to student and occasion to occasion – even question to question on a test. We are well-meaning, perhaps even altruistic, and yet we will be less effective test-givers if we are uninformed, un-thoughtful, un-systematic and without explicit principles. (Beneficence – giving students the benefit of the doubt – is not always the best answer.)

Congratulations to you! By picking up this book, you've shown yourself to be at least well-meaning and perhaps even well on your way to forming or honing your own explicit, systematic values, philosophies, and principles which will guide your test-giving.

Let's have a look at what makes tests poor and what uninformed test-givers do. To be honest, there are endless ways that tests can be poor and test-givers can be uninformed. Let's focus on a couple of central reasons.

"(Why) Do I Have to Take This Test?"

First, tests tend to be poor tests when no one's quite sure why the test is being taken. Why do you give your students tests? The most fundamental reason to give students a test is to ascertain whether they've learned what you wanted them to learn. That sounds obvious, but it is not. That sounds like a given, but it is not. That purpose is a key decision rule for you regardless of the type of assessment you are using. Think of it on a t-shirt: "Purpose is Paramount"; "The Primacy of Purpose"; "Purpose is Pre-eminent". As you are designing an assessment, as you are asking your students to study for or perform an assessment, and as you are grading the products, every time you need to make a decision, you should ask yourself, "How will this aid my ability to know what students know?" Perhaps even more revealing would be to ask yourself this corollary: "How will this aid my students' ability to show what they know?" For example, will the test be open book or not? Students take longer for open book tests because they look *everything* up. That will reduce the number of questions you can ask them. It also, in general, tests their ability to use resources and not their own reasoning or recall. Closed book exams really do drive recall and memory ... and problem-solving. So which aids your ability to know what students know and for them to show what they know?

There are other good reasons to give tests. Psychologists have known for a long time that testing drives studying, that more frequent testing often results in more learning, and that how you choose to assess students impacts how they choose to study. So using tests to drive studying and learning is also an appropriate purpose for testing. We hasten to add that assessment should be one tool, but not your only tool, for encouraging and enabling students' engagement in their own learning. The student engagement literature also suggests that assessment shouldn't be your first tool, but that's all beyond the scope of this book.

We would argue with you vociferously that at any college or university, at any level, in any class or credit-earning experience, those are *always* the top two reasons (and in that order). There are additional legitimate reasons to assess students, but they are all subsequent to, and subordinate to, those two. Assessment for selecting students into or out of subsequent courses, course development, program development, institutional accountability and reporting, accreditation needs, etc., are also legitimate, but none of those should ever overtake student learning as the primary goal of assessment inside of a course. Another way to say this is that any of those other purposes can still be served through a test which has student learning as its primary goal, and yet, if those other goals come first in your assessment thinking, it makes it harder to serve the student learning purpose.

Olivia's college is ramping up student outcomes assessment in preparation for reaccreditation. The college is going to come to her and ask for evidence that her students are meeting the learning objectives for her course and perhaps broader learning objectives tied to the Associate of Arts degree in history and the learning objectives for the college's core curriculum for all students. To oversimplify, she has two choices. She can work from the outside into her course by looking at those broad, core curriculum learning objectives and trying to add some assessment that neither she nor her students quite understand so that she has something to hand the college's assessment coordinator. She can work from the inside of her course out by articulating how those broader learning objectives are carried out specifically through her own learning objectives for the course and how she assesses them for her students and herself. The former approach is going to feel forced, disconnected, and will actually decrease Olivia's and her students' buy in to the broader learning objectives. The latter approach meets her students' learning needs first – including the broader objectives, which are now course-relevant – and still will provide the department and the college with the data they need to demonstrate that students are meeting the learning objectives.

Uninformed test-givers don't really know why they give tests, or they don't own the reasons as their own. Some test-givers give tests because, when they were a student, they took tests and so their students should, too. It's the "test unto others as others have tested unto you" rule. That's not very motivating for you, and it's definitely not motivating for your students. Some test-givers would answer a student query with the Nuremberg defense: "My department chair told me I need to give this test." While that may actually be true – you may be required to use certain assessments and/or assessment formats for reasons that are not your own – that mindset could hamper your own thinking and creativity about how you and your students can get the most out of those assessments. Voicing that reason in front of the class in response to a student question undermines your authority with your students and demotivates them. If you're not invested in the test, why should they be?

Preet is well along in fostering this understanding. Teaching statistics, especially to people who don't see it as directly part of their ultimate career goals, requires constant attention to "Why is this important?" So she is well-versed in articulating to students why showing your work or needing to memorize a formula, or being able to interpret output from statistical software is critical. She also has lots of experience justifying practice problems, exams, and class participation to students.

Uninformed test-givers espouse very proximate, learning-dampening goals to students. There are large bodies of converging research literature that can be drastically oversimplified to this statement: students who focus on, and care most about, "The Grade" and how their grades compare to their classmates' are much less effective learners than students who focus on, and care most about, "The Learning" and how they compare to themselves. Therefore when students ask you, "Why do I have to take the test?", it is more beneficial to students for you to say, "Because you and I will get a good sense of what you have learned and what you have yet to learn," than for you to say, "Because you need a good grade on this test if you want to pass the class. It is 33 percent of the final grade, you know!" In other words, uninformed test-givers give reasons that are more immediate yet more tangential to student learning: "I need to fill out your mid-semester progress reports, and I need some data." "This material will be on the licensing exam." "You have to know this stuff!" Sam honed these explanations when he chose to focus on writing in a biology class.

Unscrupulous test-givers use tests to punish students. Perhaps you've had the experience as a student with an instructor, who, after asking a few questions of the students and getting blank stares says, "OK! Pop quiz! Right now!" We did just say that using tests to steer students' studying was an appropriate use of tests. However, there are much better ways than the pop quiz (let alone the punitive pop quiz) to do that. Briefly here, and in much more detail throughout the book, it is much better to communicate with students about what the learning objectives in the course are, which are more important than others, what will be on the test, how it will be on the test, when the test will be, etc., so that students are able to make informed, strategic choices about what to study, how to study, and when to study. Pop quizzes provoke fear and anxiety, which are just not synonymous with a student-centered and learning-centered classroom. Sam will embarrassingly admit to having popped a quiz in response to blank stares, but he's much happier with using the reading journals.

Similarly, unscrupulous test-givers use tests for their own amusement or to "teach students a lesson". Jay had a high school history teacher whose name was Mr. Test (no, we're not making that up; that really was his name!). On test days, he'd stand scratching his chin through his beard and, among other instructions, tell us, "I don't believe in gimmes and I don't believe in gotchas." That is, you got his questions right because you knew the right answer and you got them wrong if you didn't, and there weren't other explanations. Gimmes are freebies like purely humorous questions, content unrelated to class: "Mickey Mouse" as an option on a multiple-choice question. Gotchas are trick questions. (Jay still thinks "Diet of Worms" as an option on one of Mr. Test's multiple-choice questions was actually a gotcha, but we'll pick that back up in a later chapter on how to write options.)

Gimmes and gotchas are problematic because they signal to students that there's a cat-and-mouse game going on, a cops-and-robbers, us-vs.-them, dynamic which draws their attention to the test itself and the grade and away from the learning that the test is supposed to be focused on. A particularly nasty version of gotchas are the "psych/double-psych" games unscrupulous test-givers play with examinees: making the correct answers to the first 10 multiple-choice questions "B" so that students are thinking about whether the instructor would or wouldn't actually do that and perhaps even changing an answer here and there to avoid that pattern.

The Latin root for the word "assessment" is "assidēre", which means "to sit beside". As assessors with a student-learning focus, we are to sit beside students, to work *with* them in this process. Gimmes and gotchas put us *against* students, in opposition to them. Olivia, Preet, and Sam each have developed their own version of the mindset of helping and aiding students with their learning rather than thinking like a cop who is trying to "catch" students.

Informed, principled test-givers, on the other hand, explicitly know the answer to the question "Why do I have to take the test?" when students ask. They know how the test fits into their overall assessment plan, course plan, and even their teaching philosophy. And, with student learning at the forefront, informed test-givers communicate early and often with students about why they are giving tests and why students are taking them.

Informed test-givers put student learning first but are also forthright with students about other purposes. It may, indeed, be true that you've chosen to include certain questions on this mid-term exam because they will ultimately be on the licensing exam students will have to take. So you can tell them that, but don't stop there. Help them see why the material itself is so valuable to the profession and to professionals in their daily lives that you and the licensing board think it's important enough to spend time on.

Thank publicly that first student in every class brazen enough to ask you, "(Why) do I have to take the test?" This student has given you the gift of the opportunity to explain to all of your students why your tests are important learning events – if you haven't already provided those explanations. Elsewhere in the book, we'll provide communication strategies for you to use to aid you in this effort. This student has also given you the gift of the reminder that you need to have an explicit answer for yourself and for your students to this question. Your answer for yourself and for them should emphasize student learning first and honestly include the other appropriate purposes.

"What Will Be on the Test?"

Second, tests tend to be poor tests when no one's quite sure what is being tested. You and your students need clear statements of learning objectives (instructional objectives, learning targets): what it is you want the students to know and be able to do. If you aren't clear about what you want students to know and be able to do, there's little chance that your students will be clear. This snowballs. If you're not clear on this, your instruction may not address what you really want. And, if you're not clear on this, your assessments likely will be, literally, off-target. While the details of how to construct strong learning objectives are beyond the scope of this book, there are some wonderful book-length and shorter treatments of this topic available. Two of the best texts are Mager's *Preparing Instructional Objectives* (1997) and Gronlund and Brookhart's *Gronlund's Writing Instructional Objectives* (2009).

Unscrupulous test-givers are poor communicators about the test. They think learning is served by withholding information from students about the test itself. There's a corollary to "What will be on the test?", which is, "How will we be tested?" Some test-givers incorrectly think they're "giving away the test" by telling students things like what kinds of items will be on the test; how much time will students have to take the test; will it be open book or not; etc. Actually, providing students with such information communicates importance and priority to them – important learning goals in their own right – and helps to guide their learning away from purely measurement-related issues (e.g. should they guess or leave an item blank) and on to substantive issues (e.g. why is chapter 12 more central to the field than chapter 11). We will discuss methods for communicating with your students about these issues.

"We Didn't Cover This in Class!!!!"

The third reason is that tests tend to be poor tests when they're loosely related (or unrelated!) to instruction. There are actually three ways in which the connection between instruction and assessment slips. Content mismatches are one way. Have you heard a student allege, post-exam during your office hours, "But we didn't cover this in class!"? That's a content mismatch: when something which wasn't addressed in class (or in readings, homework assignments, etc.) appears on the test. Second, the way you want students to know something can change from instruction to assessment. If you emphasize use of a formula in class but on the exam students have to have it memorized, that represents a "way of knowing" mismatch. Third, the proportion of content is a little more subtle yet likely more common than the other two mismatches. This happens when you've spent, perhaps, 20 percent of instructional time on a particular concept, yet it constitutes 40 percent of the exam.

Some unscrupulous test-givers erroneously try to exploit this mismatch to drive learning. Let's take the proportion of content as an example. If the upcoming exam is going to cover chapters 11–15, chances are those chapters were not covered equally in instruction (20 percent of instructional time per chapter) and won't be covered equally on the exam (20 percent of questions or points per chapter). I've heard college instructors say they wouldn't tell students what the actual exam proportions were, though, because "It's all important, and I want them to know it all." That is untrue or the exam would indeed be 20 percent per chapter. It wastes students' study time and effort. And it fails to communicate to students that, indeed, some of the content *is* more important than other content. We devote an entire chapter to a useful tool for aiding this alignment called the *test blueprint*.

In summary, we hold that students don't hate tests, they hate poor tests, and they don't respect uninformed test-givers. Poor tests and uninformed test-givers do not focus solely on student learning. In order truly to pull these ideas together, we have to ask you a highly personal question: Are you a test-giver or an educator?

Are You a Test-Giver or an Educator?

One of our bedrock principles is that there are no boundaries between instruction, learning, and assessment. All can happen simultaneously. Pull a coin out of your pocket. No, really, we'll wait. Notice that your coin clearly has a "heads" side to it (like Instruction); and it clearly has a "tails" side to it (like Assessment). Now turn it in your hand so you're looking at the edge of the coin. See if you can find the place where "heads" stops and "tails" starts; where the two halves were pressed together. Yes, we do know that heads and tails are stamped onto a single metal disc and are not assembled of two halves. That's actually our main point here: instruction and assessment are like that. They *are* the same thing but have different faces. It is very difficult to determine when one stops and the other begins even though there are plenty of times when you can point clearly to one or the other. Both are learning. So we are *never* test-givers only. We cannot be *just* test-givers. If we are truly interested in student learning as the primary outcome, and we understand that learning is driven by both instruction and assessment, then we must see ourselves as educators not only as test-givers when we are thinking about our assessor functions. A test-giver only cannot be an educator. There is a role in education, generally, and in society, more generally, for stand-alone test-giving. Those functions, though, are not those of someone who has primary responsibility for working with a group of learners.

Uninformed test-givers think that assessment is what happens after instruction stops; that there is no connection between them; that students couldn't possibly learn anything during or after the assessment. This is the "dipstick" approach: that tests are a dipstick plunged into the amount of student learning, a dipstick which doesn't affect that which it is measuring. Such test-givers change identity around test-time, and they start engaging in learning-dampening behaviors, because they are "The Tester".

Educators are mindful of the entire coin the entire time. If they're teaching, they're thinking about assessment implications, and when they're assessing, they're attuned to the instruction. Let's put this all together more formally in the formative assessment cycle.

The Formative Assessment Cycle

Educators understand the instruction and assessment cycle with feedback as a connector (depicted in Figure 1.1). Formative assessment is assessment which leads to additional learning, to further instruction. Some instructional or learning event happens, which is followed by some assessment; from which feedback informs more instruction and/or learning.

In order for the cycle to turn over – to spin – all three activities have to happen. Feedback is often the missing piece. If Preet gives a mid-term exam and posts exam scores to the web-based gradebook for students to check, there is very little, if any, feedback which will result in further learning. Remember those papers in the trash can at the end of the hall where your office is? You provided feedback, but the students didn't absorb it. If feedback falls in the hallway, does anybody hear it? Even if they read it before they threw it away, why did they throw it away? Because no additional learning or assessment was coming. Feedback is most valuable when it points forward to the next "performance", which implies that the formative assessment cycle will "spin".

We understand that time is a finite resource and that instructors and learners must move on to other topics. But there are ways, even so, to provide for the "next" performance. One way is actually a change of perspective. As we've already mentioned, if you and your students are grade focused, and/or

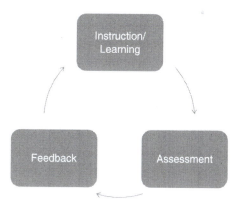

Figure 1.1 The Formative Assessment Cycle

short-term focused, then reading the feedback on the paper or looking to see which questions were missed on the test, and why, are low-yield activities. But if you and your students have a learning focus, and/or a long-term focus – these skills will be important to you on the job – then there remains a next performance but it's beyond the end of the semester. Another way is to provide feedback which focuses not on the specific learning in *this* assessment but to some broader skill. For example, perhaps Olivia has a semester-long goal for students to improve their use of sources when they write the end-of-term paper, or Preet wants her students to learn certain problem-solving strategies which they used on the test. If Olivia's feedback to them points them forward to their use of sources in their next paper – even though the content of the paper will be very different – or if Preet's feedback points them forward to the problems they'll need to solve on the next exam, it raises the yield for students of attending to their feedback. A third approach is to build opportunities for students to revisit a test or to turn in another draft of the paper incorporating instructor feedback. Feedback is most valuable when it clearly points to the next performance, and the "next performance" may be a matter of perspective, a matter of course design, and/or an occasion you construct for your students.

It's important to know that this cycle can spin at various speeds. When you say something in class, notice confused looks on half of the faces, and you make the point a different way, you've seen all three phases of the formative assessment cycle in a matter of seconds. If you give students a 10-item quiz at the end of class on Tuesday; post scores online and suggest some additional practice problems prior to class on Thursday; and then reteach those concepts in class on Thursday, the cycle spun in three days. The rps (revolutions per semester) of this cycle are important to attend to. The faster this cycle spins for students, the more times it can spin during a given instructional period. And the more frequently it turns over, the more student learning will be advanced. Preet will be thrilled to learn in later chapters how well the online environment can be constructed to facilitate this. So we want to look for ways to turn this over not just powerfully and effectively but also quickly and efficiently.

In this book, we will look at ways to provide feedback in MCQ contexts. We'll also examine ways to provide additional learning and assessment opportunities for students so that their feedback can impact a next learning. And we'll examine ways to be more efficient at all of the elements of the cycle.

The Plan for this Book

This book is presented in four sections. Section 1 is about writing test questions with a chapter on the multiple-choice question itself and another on variations on multiple-choice questions. Most test question formats where students select an answer, like true/false and matching, are actually variations on multiple choice. With those fundamentals down, we move on in Section 2 to address how to build and use tests themselves. A test is far from being just a long list of questions! Section 3 articulates how to appropriate technology for assessment and for learning through multiple-choice questions. Finally, Section 4 describes what you and your students can be doing before, during, and after a test to keep the learning moving forward.

Take a Deep Seat and a Far-Off Gaze

There's an expression in Texas: "Take a deep seat and a far-off gaze." We quote it here as a reminder to take a long view of your assessment practice, specifically, and your teaching more generally. We're going to discuss lots and lots of strategies in this book. Many of them could become a sabbatical-sized project to implement with full complexity and rigor. We owe it to you to state explicitly that we do not expect you to tackle all of them at once (or any of them at once!). In fact, we do not expect you to jump into any course with all of these suggestions and ideas we're discussing in this book fully implemented. Don't hurt yourself! Choose some baseline, basic concepts that you'll employ, and then layer on others as you go, semester after semester. Item banking is a great example: start with a basic set of items and try to increase the bank each semester you teach the class. For security reasons, for item quality reasons, and because courses grow and change, you will likely be retiring some items while adding others. That's perfectly fine. In Jay's first year as an assistant professor, a senior colleague observed him teaching. At the debrief session, the senior colleague was working through a list of things that went really well. Jay said, "OK. But let's get to that list of stuff that needs to be better!" The senior colleague said only, "Teach that course five more times." In the subsequent years of experience Jay has had, the richness and wisdom of that feedback has only gotten deeper. So take it easy on yourself and teach it five more times, adding and refining as you go. Take a deep seat and a far-off gaze because, like the cattle-drives of yore, this is going to be a long but ultimately profitable ride.

Conclusion

MCQs and multiple-choice tests can be rich learning experiences for you and your students as well as rich assessment experiences. If you approach testing as an educator who knows why you're testing, what is on the test, and how that relates to what happens in class, you are well on your way to having meaningful assessment experiences with your students. From here, we'll look at several techniques and practices which you can use to achieve these ends.

Again, congratulations on choosing multiple-choice testing for you and your students and for showing sufficient curiosity about the possibility of using it to promote learning among your students. Let's get started!

References and Resources for Further Reading

Gronlund, N. E. and Brookhart, S. M. (2009). *Gronlund's Writing Instructional Objectives.* Upper Saddle River, NJ: Pearson/Merrill Prentice Hall.

Mager, R. F. (1997). *Preparing Instructional Objectives: A critical tool in the development of effective instruction* (3rd ed.). Atlanta, GA: The Center for Effective Performance, Inc.

Section I

Writing Multiple-Choice Questions

2 The Basic Multiple-Choice Question

Like so many things in life, the ubiquity of multiple-choice questions around us provides us with a false sense of familiarity. We know them, sure, but how well do we really know them? Kind of like social media "friends". Let us begin, then, by making sure we understand just what a multiple-choice question is, then we can move on to what makes a good MCQ.

Anatomy of a Multiple-Choice Question

Reader, this is a multiple-choice question (MCQ). MCQ, this is our reader. This, and most of the other items in this chapter, are from Professor Shah's introductory statistics course (see Figure 2.1).

Now that we have the basic introduction down, let's get better acquainted. The initial part of a MCQ which most examinees read first is called the *stem*. It's referred to as the stem and not the question because, in some instances, it is a statement not a question. The stem is the task put before the examinee. It lays out the premise for the MCQ, provides information, and sometimes misinformation, and perhaps even some directions for how to think about the answer. Below the stem is a series of options from which the examinee is asked to select an answer. The option which is the correct answer is called the *key* and the other options are *distractors*.

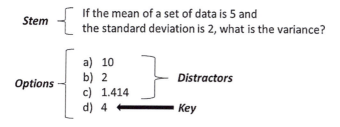

Figure 2.1 The Parts of a Multiple-Choice Question

What is the measure of central tendency most susceptible to the effects of extreme values?

    a) mean**

    b) standard deviation

    c) kurtosis

    d) sum

What is the measure of central tendency most susceptible to the effects of extreme values?

    a) mean**

    b) median

    c) mode

    d) sum

Figure 2.2 Correct Option Versus Best Option MCQs

There are some basic variations on the MCQ which we should discuss immediately. (There are also some not-so-basic variations which we will examine in the next chapter.) Look at Figure 2.2 carefully.

The two stems are identical but the options are different. The first item is an example of a *correct option* MCQ. In a correct option MCQ, there is one option which is unambiguously correct and the distractors are unambiguously incorrect. In this item the mean is the measure of central tendency most susceptible to the effects of extreme values and is also the *only* measure of central tendency among the options. (Standard deviation is a measure of variation; kurtosis is a measure of distribution shape; and sum is the addition of all values in the data set.) The second item is an example of a *best option* MCQ. In a best option MCQ, there is one option which is the most correct, or best, and the distractors might be correct in some sense but are not the most correct. In the second item in the figure, mean, median, and mode are all measures of central tendency but mean is the most susceptible of the three to extreme values.

Your students would prefer that you employ correct option MCQs because these items tend to be less ambiguous and thus easier to answer. You might prefer them because they cut down on student complaints about the questions and the exam. You are more likely to prefer best option MCQs because, when you're feeling deeply principled, they require finer distinctions in thinking from your students, and when you're feeling exhausted writing items, they're easier for you to write because the format can bear some ambiguity.

Regardless of which format you select and why, always tell your students, in study guides as well as in the directions for the test, which kind you are using on the test. It is best not to mix and match them; although, if you're going to do that, instruct students which ones are best option MCQs.

Distractors Are Not Tricks; They're Good Measurement

You may be wondering why the non-key options are called distractors. Some test-givers mistakenly think that non-key options are passive camouflage whose job is to hide the key. Distractors are there to do an active job – several active jobs really. First, distractors are there to entice examinees who don't know or aren't sure what the key is to select them. Yes, you read that right, "entice", and yet this isn't a trick. There is a real measurement purpose at work.

In our first chapter, we strongly defined the primary purpose of giving a test to be finding out whether or not students have mastered the learning objectives. So our MCQs need to provide us with information on that very issue: Do they know what they are supposed to know? A distractor's active role is to further that goal; that is, a distractor is to entice an examinee who doesn't know what they are supposed to know into selecting the distractor, not the key. If such a student selects the key, we've got poor information. So this isn't tricking students; it's effective measurement.

In order to perform that measurement job, distractors need to be *plausible* – believable to the student who doesn't quite know the material well enough. We've all seen or heard of "Mickey Mouse" appearing as an option. Unless Mickey is content-relevant, he's not a plausible distractor. It's actually better measurement to have fewer options on a MCQ than the MCQs around it in the test than to have it have the same number of options, some of which are implausible. We could reasonably debate the inclusion of "d) sum" in the second item in Figure 2.2 on these grounds since it isn't a measure of central tendency. Might the question actually be better with only three options?

Plausibility needs to be viewed from the perspective of the examinee to some extent. In Chapter 1, we mentioned Jay's high school history teacher, Mr. Test, who used "Diet of Worms" as a distractor. As you may recall, the Diet of Worms was a gathering of officials of the Holy Roman Empire in 1521 which had a large impact on Martin Luther's career path. Jay doesn't actually remember what the content of the test was about but it wasn't the Reformation. So to a group of teenagers who hadn't studied these historical events, it sounded like a description of what fish eat. That, then, was totally implausible to us as a potential key on the item. Jay will freely admit that it so struck his imagination that he either asked what it was or looked it up and still remembers it to this day. Some instructors might say, "See, that had learning value!" We totally agree; it did. Jay mastered the distractor but has forgotten the learning objective! That doesn't justify using such things on tests. That distractor was not related to the learning objective, which is the learning we are responsible for promoting. That distractor had little measurement value.

So how do you come up with plausible distractors? Draw on your students' misconceptions and mistakes. Let's return to Figure 2.1 for a moment. First, let us remind you that the standard deviation of a set of values is the square root of the variance; that's the learning this item is meant to measure. The four options were not generated out of thin air; rather, each has its own justification for being here. Option "a) 10" is the mean times the standard deviation value in the stem. This is probably what a student would select who understood nearly nothing about the actual content but, figuring some mathematical function is required, puts the two numbers from the stem together in a way that produces one of the options. This probably represents a wild guess. Option "b) 2" assumes that the standard deviation and the variance are synonymous. This is an uncommon but not improbable mistake of introductory statistics students. Option "c) 1.414" represents the square root of the standard deviation. This will catch the student who reverses the relationship between variance and standard deviation or the student who knows something needs to be square-rooted but doesn't remember exactly what. Option "d) 4" is the key, the square of the standard deviation.

Another reason that plausible distractors are good measurement – and great for learning – is that they are diagnostic. If a student selects a distractor instead of the key, and you have created that distractor from a particular mistake or misconception, then you can be reasonably sure the student held that misconception or made that mistake. This is valuable information for the student to have (and we'll write at length later about student feedback) to understand what they yet need to learn. It is also valuable information for you in the aggregate. If 27 percent of your students selected 1.414, then perhaps you should review the mathematical relationship between variance and standard deviation. Again, there'll more later on techniques for you to use to gain these insights.

With that basic introduction, we can now look at best practices for building your own, or evaluating someone else's, MCQs.

A Framework for Item-Writing

There are dozens of rules for writing MCQs and lots of different lists of rules (e.g. Haladyna *et al.*, 2002). Some of the rules are common sense (e.g. MCQs should be free of spelling and grammatical errors), some of them less so (e.g. avoid "All of the above").

Inevitably with so many rules and lists of rules, they overlap or sound similar, creating a rather jumbled mess. So what is an item-writer like yourself to do? Here, rather than promoting our own favorite flavors and expressions of the rules, we would like to offer you a framework for thinking about item-writing into which most, if not all, of the rules you're ever likely to run across will fall. When you are writing your own items, you should be attending to *validity concerns* and *cognitive load concerns*.

Table 2.1 A Revised Taxonomy of Multiple-Choice Item-Writing Guidelines

Content concerns

1. Every item should reflect specific content and a single specific mental behavior, as called for in test specifications (two-way grid, test blueprint).
2. Base each item on important content to learn; avoid trivial content.
3. Use novel material to test higher level learning. Paraphrase textbook language or language used during instruction when used in a test item to avoid testing for simply recall.
4. Keep the content of each item independent from content of other items on the test.
5. Avoid over specific and over general content when writing MC items.
6. Avoid opinion-based items.
7. Avoid trick items.
8. Keep vocabulary simple for the group of students being tested.

Formatting concerns

9. Use the question, completion, and best answer versions of the conventional MC, the alternate choice, true-false (TF), multiple true-false (MTF), matching, and the context-dependent item and item set formats, but AVOID the complex MC (Type K) format.
10. Format the item vertically instead of horizontally.

Style concerns

11. Edit and proof items.
12. Use correct grammar, punctuation, capitalization, and spelling.
13. Minimize the amount of reading in each item.

Writing the stem

14. Ensure that the directions in the stem are very clear.
15. Include the central idea in the stem instead of the choices.
16. Avoid window dressing (excessive verbiage).
17. Word the stem positively; avoid negatives such as NOT or EXCEPT. If negative words are used, use the word cautiously and always ensure that the word appears capitalized and boldface.

Writing the choices

18. Develop as many effective choices as you can, but research suggests three is adequate.
19. Make sure that only one of these choices is the right answer.
20. Vary the location of the right answer according to the number of choices.
21. Place choices in logical or numerical order.
22. Keep choices independent; choices should not be overlapping.
23. Keep choices homogeneous in content and grammatical structure.
24. Keep the length of choices about equal.
25. *None of the above* should be used carefully.
26. Avoid *All of the above.*
27. Phrase choices positively; avoid negatives such as NOT.
28. Avoid giving clues to the right answer, such as
    a. Specific determiners including always, never, completely, and absolutely.
    b. Clang associations, choices identical to or resembling words in the stem.
    c. Grammatical inconsistencies that cue the test-taker to the correct choice.
    d. Conspicuous correct choice.
    e. Pairs or triplets of options that clue the test-taker to the correct choice.
    f. Blatantly absurd, ridiculous options.
29. Make all distractors plausible.
30. Use typical errors of students to write your distractors.
31. Use humor if it is compatible with the teacher and the learning environment.

Source: Haladyna et al. (2002). Reprinted by permission of the publisher (Taylor & Francis Ltd, www.tandfonline.com).

Validity concerns revolve around what is actually measured by a MCQ. You're trying to find out if students understand how $F = ma$ contributes to low speed automobile collisions in your physics course but perhaps your overreliance on jargon makes it hard for students to know what you're actually asking. So whether they get the question right or not hinges on their verbal skills rather than on their understanding of $F = ma$. Validity concerns impinge on what the score means when students are done with the test. Why did they get the question right (or wrong)? Perhaps they got the question right because they guessed "B". Many item-writing rules promote valid responses to MCQs and/or try to head off invalid responses.

Cognitive load concerns involve what students are spending their thinking time thinking about while they're taking the test. Your students shouldn't have to think harder than the content requires. They should also be thinking about the tested content, not about the process of taking the test.

These two concerns are appropriate for writing individual items; they're also appropriate for designing the entire test itself. We'll address the latter later. With those two concerns in mind, let's examine some of the specific item-writing rules to see how these concerns play out.

Avoid Window Dressing

Window dressing in a MCQ is information in the item itself which is superfluous to the content being assessed and to the assessment process itself. Have a look at the two items in Figure 2.3. The first item contains window

---

Professor of Psychiatry, R. U. Nutz, was intrigued by the number of times his anxiety patients used the word "worried" during his 50-minute sessions with them. He started counting the numbers of times 15 of his patients used that word or a derivative (e.g. "worry", "worrier", etc.) during their sessions. He computed the mean for this set of data to be 5 and the standard deviation is 2. What is the variance of these data?

    a) 10

    b) 2

    c) 1.414

    d) 4**

If the mean of a set of data is 5 and the standard deviation is 2, what is the variance?

    a) 10

    b) 2

    c) 1.414

    d) 4**

Figure 2.3 Window Dressing

dressing. Who is doing the study, what he is studying, who he is studying have no bearing on the relationship between variance and standard deviation. All of that information adds extraneous information which may confuse students as to the point of the question (a validity concern) and definitely causes them to spend time reading and deciding on the relevance of the information (a cognitive load concern) in which they don't actually need to engage in order to answer the question.

Given our definition of window dressing, this isn't just about shorter stems versus longer stems; it's about the relevance of what is there. Shorter stems are not *ipso facto* better. If the details are relevant to the learning objective, then length is acceptable. The other aspect of our definition to note is whether the details, even superfluous ones, serve an assessment purpose. Sometimes the learning objective is that students will be able to sort relevant from irrelevant information in solving a problem. In that case, superfluous details are necessary. We'll return to these issues in the next chapter when we discuss vignette-based MCQs.

Don't Copy and Paste Language from Elsewhere Directly into the Test Question

One of Jay's favorite quotes about writing in general is from Gene Fowler: "Writing is easy: All you do is sit staring at a blank sheet of paper until drops of blood form on your forehead." Item-writing can be a particularly excruciating type of writing. Thus, we look for shortcuts. For example, perhaps we need an example of a concept and the physics course textbook has that very succinctly articulated example of train crossings as low speed but high force collisions. Why can't we simply cut and paste that example out of the book onto the test? Our objection isn't copyright, because there are legal ways to use others' materials in our tests. We have a cognitive load and perhaps a validity concern with this practice. Small amounts of text taken out of their original context sometimes don't read the same or aren't as clear. It's entirely possible that the example of train crossings makes sense because it was in the middle of page 217 of the textbook and benefited from having followed page 216. So what is clear in the textbook isn't always clear out of that context. You also want to consider the validity of the student's response. Likely your student learning outcome for such a question would be something like: "The student will be able to recognize examples of each of the following concepts ..." If you're giving them an example from the book, are they really meeting that learning outcome or are they remembering that example because it was in the book? Better all the way around to create your own examples. You can use the one in the book as a template from which you pull some details and add others, but there is value in not copying directly from course materials.

Watch Your Language

The actual language you use in your MCQs can become cognitive load and validity concerns. We've already discussed superfluous language, and we used jargon as an example. Another issue is the linguistic complexity of your items in general. You should write your questions using the language appropriate to the learning objectives of the course, appropriate to your profession, and appropriate to your students' academic level and position relative to the profession. It is inappropriate to be pretentious with professional language or to use language deliberately above the reading level of the students. Every aspect of the MCQ, including the language, needs to be appropriate for the students and for the learning objectives.

One of our favorite examples of this is a study (Abedi and Lord, 2001) of math test questions for upper elementary students. The researchers took math problems with a fair bit of language load and created a version where the math stayed the same but the reading level was well below the grade level of the students. The main focus of the study was to see if the language simplification aided English Language Learners in showing their mathematics knowledge, although the researchers included non-ELLs in the study, too. The final result was fascinating and very relevant to our point: *all students*, not just the ELLs, did better when the language was simplified.

We are not arguing for simplifying all language all of the time. There are times when complex language is relevant to the learning objectives and/or professionally appropriate to the students. Such linguistic complexity is totally appropriate. The item-writing rule articulates that the language should be no more complex than it has to be.

Another language-related rule is to use negative words sparingly. First, words and statements of negation are cognitively more difficult to process than affirmative words and statements. They require mental flipping or transposing of positives and negatives. Use a stem like "Which of the following is an example of ..." rather than a stem like "Which of the following is NOT an example of ...". Second, the negatives are easy for test-takers to miss, which makes all the difference, and creates a validity concern. They'll get the item wrong because they misread it, not because they didn't know the content. Notice the rule doesn't forbid negation words in items. If you're going to use them, mitigate the validity concerns by making the negation words hard to miss by underlining, boldfacing, capitalizing, and/or italicizing them. You can also include a note in verbal or written instructions to students to watch for the negative words.

Uninformed test-givers like negation on two counts. First, they say, "Well, they should be reading more carefully!" Yes, they should, but that's not your specific learning objective on this test and so it should not be influencing their score. Second, be aware also that negation is an item-writer's crutch.

Sometimes it's easier to think of things that are rather than things that are not, and so we chuck in a negative to save us the trouble.

Stem-Twisting

Cognitive load concerns have some other implications for the form of the stem. Look at the items in Figure 2.4.

The first version is a direct question. The following two versions are incomplete statements with a blank. Direct questions are cognitively straightforward because a test-taker holds the stem in working memory and matches options to it. An incomplete statement with the blank at the end of the stem is as cognitively straightforward as a direct question. An incomplete statement with the blank in the middle means examinees need to hold the pre-blank portion of the stem and the post-blank portion of the stem in working memory and then place each option in between. That's hard. Alternatively, an examinee has to use time to create a series of true/false statements by putting option A into the blank and asking "true or false"? If "false", then try option B, and so forth. The rule then is to use direct questions or, if you're using incomplete statements, put the blank at the end of the statement. While either approach is acceptable, writing the stem in the form of a question generally results in a clearer item than incomplete statements.

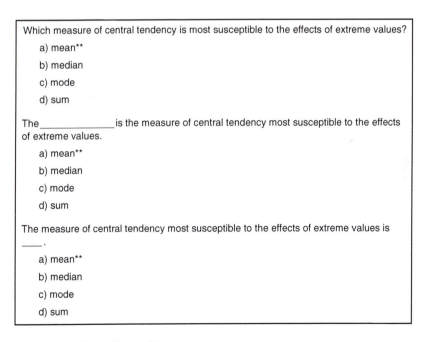

Figure 2.4 Different Types of Stems

In a normal distribution, 95% of the observations are enclosed _____.

  a) within one-and-a-half standard deviations of the mean

  b) within two standard deviations of the mean

  c) within three standard deviations of the mean

  d) within four standard deviations of the mean

In a normal distribution, 95% of the observations are enclosed within _____ standard deviations of the mean.

  a) one-and-a-half

  b) two

  c) three

  d) four

Figure 2.5 Put Repeated Words in the Stem

Another cognitive load rule is to put repeated words in the stem, not in the options. Take a look at Figure 2.5.

You've noticed that we've preferenced the blank in the middle over the blank at the end, contradicting the point we just made. The issue, in the end, is cognitive load: which version is harder in total for the examinee to think about. In Figure 2.5, putting the blank at the end necessitates lots of repeated words in the options, words that an examinee not only needs to read but also needs to read carefully checking for subtle discrepancies. By putting the repeated words in the stem, they are only processed once. Written in question form, the item might read: "In a normal distribution, 95 percent of the observations are enclosed within how many standard deviations of the mean?" Admittedly, these processes we're describing take milliseconds, and yet cognitive effort is cognitive effort.

The Key is Key

When writing the key, there are two rules. First, the key should be unambiguously correct. It cannot be mostly correct, or sort of correct, it has to be correct. Second, the key needs to represent some consensus of the field. You should be able to point to an external source like the textbook, a reading the students have done, or a set of professional standards, etc. These are validity issues because they point to the meaning of the score. Did the student get the item right because they could read your mind or did they get it right because they know the content that is important to the field?

It's Nice to Have Options

Writing options can be one of the hardest parts of item-writing. Let's begin by easing the burden a little bit. We alluded to this earlier: the measurement properties of your scores will not be affected, by and large, by using items with different numbers of options. The benefits of forcing all items to have four or five options are often outweighed by the costs of the implausible distractors or other tortured options you produce in order to create a constant number of options. Put more plainly, it's better that all items have solid, plausible options than that they all have the same number of options. The one place number of options matters is in the probability that students could guess the item correct; however, if you use "Mickey Mouse" as an option so that all your items have four options, how is that truly different from three options only? Rodriguez (2005) analyzed 80 years of research on the best number of options to use in a multiple-choice question and the overwhelming evidence suggests that three options (key and two distractors) works just as well as questions with four or five options where some of the distractors are ineffective. In general, write as many *plausible* options that align to student misconceptions as you can without exceeding a total of five options. Now that we've eased the burden, here are some other important considerations for writing options.

One of the rules for writing option sets is to order the options meaningfully. In Figures 2.5 and 2.6, we have listed the options in numerical order. This is important cognitively because examinees are predisposed to expect lists to be in a meaningful order: numerically, alphabetically, chronologically, left to right, west to east, etc. It is important for validity, too, because we are so strongly predisposed to expect a meaningful order that we will put them in that order mentally whether they actually are or not. If we had the options in Figures 2.5 and 2.6 out of numerical order, someone who knew the answer was "two" may well pick B whether "two" is next to B or not because it should be the second choice. Later we'll discuss strategies in online assessment that allow you to easily do things like scramble the option order. You'll need to balance your reasons for wanting to do something like that (e.g. to combat cheating with online assessments) with the potential impact on cognitive load when the order might not make sense.

It is tempting for lots of reasons to want to save space by presenting options as tandem sets (bottom of Figure 2.6) instead of as lists (top of Figure 2.6).

Tandem sets introduce validity issues because examinees invariably misread them, thinking the options are ordered left to right instead of up and down. Or they fail to see the inside list at all. Tandem sets create more problems than they solve.

Your keen eye has noticed that we are always using letters for options and not numbers, Roman numerals, or other characters. We employ the convention of using Arabic numerals for items and lower case alphabetic characters for options. This prevents the cognitive load and validity concern of students needing to keep option numbers and item numbers distinct.

Another validity issue with options is their length. As an item-writer who has just been told to make the key unambiguously correct, you might try to

---

In a normal distribution, 95% of the observations are enclosed within _____ standard deviations of the mean.

   a) one-and-a-half

   b) two**

   c) three

   d) four

In a normal distribution, 95% of the observations are enclosed within _____ standard deviations of the mean.

a) one-and-a-half	c) three
b) two**	d) four

Figure 2.6 Use Lists Not Tandem Sets

do so by adding information to the key to make it unambiguous. But when you do that, item after item after item, examinees can catch on, even unconsciously, that the long one is usually the key. That's a form of what cognitive psychologists call cueing. Length of option becomes a cue to the examinee about the key.

Cueing also arises in another common item-writer's trap: "All of the above" and "None of the above". For item-writers, creating lots of plausible options is very difficult. It's sometimes a crutch to lob a "None of the above" in to fill in an option. But item-writers tend to use "All of the above" only when that is the key and "None of the above" as an extra option. When "All of the above" is the correct answer, students only need partial knowledge to get the question correct. For example, if there are five options with the fifth option being "All of the above", students only need to know that two of the four options are correct to know that "All of the above" is the correct answer. Similarly, if students can eliminate one of the options they can also eliminate "All of the above" as the correct answer, making guessing among the remaining options easier. When "None of the above" is used as the key, you have not truly assessed the learning objective being covered in the question. For these reasons, the prevailing wisdom is to avoid "All of the above" and "None of the above" as options.

Summary

So there you have the basic introduction to the multiple-choice question. Each part of the MCQ has a job to do and needs to be constructed with those jobs in mind. What the score ultimately means (i.e. validity issues) and what examinees are thinking about when responding to the item (i.e. cognitive load issues) are important organizing principles when writing MCQs.

References and Resources for Further Reading

Abedi, J. and Lord, C. (2001). The language factor in mathematics tests. *Applied Measurement in Education*, 14(3), 219–34.

Haladyna, T. M., Downing, S. M., and Rodriguez, M. C. (2002). A review of multiple-choice item-writing guidelines for classroom assessment. *Applied Measurement in Education*, 15(3), 309–34.

Rodriguez, M. C. (2005). Three options are optimal for multiple-choice items: A meta-analysis of 80 years of research. *Educational Measurement: Issues and Practice*, 24(2), 3–13.

3   Variations and Elaborations

Now that you've got the basic multiple-choice item down, we can examine some variations and elaborations of it. We'll look at variations that include reusing the same set of options repeatedly (matching items), reducing the number of options to just two (alternative choice or binary choice items), linking several MCQs together into a set (context-dependent item sets), and expanding the stem to several sentences (vignette-based MCQs).

MCQs are part of a broader set of test item types called supplied response or selected response item formats that are actually special cases of MCQs. These names are used because the answer is "supplied" by the test-maker and the examinee's task is to locate (i.e. "select") and report it. MCQs, true/false, and matching items are all common examples. (Sometimes when students are grumbling about taking a multiple-choice test, Jay will say, "What could be easier? The answers are on the test!" They don't actually appreciate hearing that.) The other item type is constructed response, where the examinee has to construct the answer. These include fill-in-the-blank, short essay, long essay, projects, papers, portfolios, etc.

There are many reasons for ringing changes on the basic multiple-choice format. First of all, making alterations widens the assessment scope we can reach: for example, by permitting a broader set of learning objectives and taxonomic levels to be addressed. We'll see several examples of this as we go.

Second, making alterations provides some solutions to item-writing conundrums endemic to the basic MCQ. For example, an item-writer's urge to write "All of the above" or "None of the above" options usually signals that there's some list involved. Perhaps a matching exercise or multiple true/false would be a better way to handle that content.

Third, by altering – but not eliminating – the basic multiple-choice format, we can harness the advantages of it. The import for you is that most of the best practice guidelines for writing MCQs also apply to these other item types like true/false and matching. We want you to be fully aware of this so that you can harness other formats to achieve good assessment in your courses.

Fourth, these permutations promote a greater authenticity in our assessments. Inauthenticity is a common criticism of MCQs. After all, when in life are we presented with four clean choices? And there's so much more to know than just the facts. It might prove helpful as we examine these formats to talk about authenticity in two different ways. One aspect of authenticity is *fidelity* – the extent to which a simulation looks like that which is being simulated. For classroom assessment, though, the much more important aspect to authenticity is whether examinees are thinking on the exam in the same ways they would be thinking in an actual situation. Alternatively – because this is *not* the same – are they thinking in ways that align with our course learning objectives? The two are different because Sam Oliver, Professor of Biology, would not expect the students in his upper division undergraduate course in ecology to be as sophisticated in their understandings of how to conduct a population density study as he would his Master's level students, and yet both can get out in the field and collect data.

Let's take a look, then, at the variety of possibilities for altering the basic multiple-choice item. While other supplied response item types are sufficiently related to MCQs for many MCQ-writing issues to apply, they are sufficiently different to require some additional best practice guidelines for each item type.

Matching Exercises

Boston in the early 1770s was a tense place to be for each individual there because it was the epicenter of the earthquake whose massive fault lines would ultimately separate the American colonies from Great Britain, and yet many of those events occurred in about one square mile of what was then very nearly an island. Olivia Peña loves to put the grand themes of the founding of the United States into the microcosm of Boston in the early 1770s because it humanizes the issues while still focusing on those issues. Nearly all of the issues and many of the actual people which would become the American Revolution were there in a small space in a relatively short time. She likes to teach with books like David Hackett Fischer's *Paul Revere's Ride* and Nathaniel Philbrick's *Bunker Hill: A City, A Siege, A Revolution* because they illustrate those forces and those people, all crammed together, so powerfully. This approach marries the enduring interest in these historical figures, places, and events with the deep educational need to grasp the various forces at work inside what is known as the American Revolution.

So it is important to Olivia that her students understand the people *and* their ideas. One of her learning objectives for this section of the course is that students will be able to articulate the various factions and their positions on important issues. Come exam time, trying to get at this with MCQs creates some challenges. What she really would like to do is give a list of several different people representing various factions or viewpoints and then a list of statements or actions to see if students could map one onto the other. Using MCQs, this would take up much testing real estate, and it would be clunky. Stems would have to be formed for each statement or action and then options

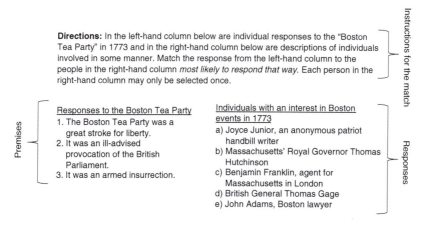

Figure 3.1 An Example of a Matching Exercise (Answers: 1) a; 2) c; 3) b).

would consist of different people and factions. It would be very repetitive. This is a great place for a matching exercise because it would cover lots of content more quickly and efficiently than MCQs could do (see Figure 3.1).

Let us spend some time with Figure 3.1. First, there are three main parts to a matching exercise: the instructions or directions; the premises (in the left-hand column); and the responses (in the right-hand column). The instructions explicitly tell examinees what the basis for the match is. They also convey other pertinent information which influences how examinees think about and through the exercise, like whether responses may only be used once or repeatedly. The premises are usually the longer, more complicated part of the exercise – the definitions, the examples, etc. The premises are also the *items*. Each one counts as a separate item or question on the test. These are analogous to the stems in a MCQ. The responses are usually the shorter, more straightforward part – the terms, the concepts, the people, etc. The responses are analogous to the options in a MCQ.

There is opportunity here for great variation. The premises and responses don't need to be verbal; they could be photographs or audio files. There could be a graph or table which frames the entire exercise.

The overarching concepts of cognitive load concerns and validity concerns are still operating here, and most of the MCQ best practice guidelines still apply. In addition, there are some additional guidelines. First, each of the two columns in a matching exercise should have substantive column headings (not Column A and Column B). Providing substantive headings (e.g. "Individuals with an interest in Boston events in 1773") aids students to understand the basis for the match they're supposed to be using. It also can cut cognitive load since they're not needing to refer back to the instructions. Second, there should be more responses than premises. If there are the same number of responses and premises, then the examinee's last choice is made through the process of elimination, not through knowledge of the content. Responses should be ordered logically, just like options on a MCQ should be.

Matching exercises work really well for lower taxonomic thinking, which we need to use the blueprint to control. While writing matching exercises, it can raise the taxonomic level of the exercise if you use novel examples or scenarios for the premises or responses rather than ones that students have seen before.

One of the tensions that can arise when using matching exercises comes between the efficiency of the format, which leads us to want to put lots of premises and responses, and the meaningfulness of the sets, which leads us to write more homogeneous sets and thus fewer sets. It is thus more important that the sets of premises and responses be meaningful, so it is likely better to write a second matching exercise than trying to squeeze multiple issues in here. For example, Olivia's matching exercise in Figure 3.1 focuses on the Boston Tea Party, but, to build a more complex view of Boston at the time, she could also be asking about other events: the Boston Massacre (1770); the Powder Alarm (1774); the John Malcolm tarring and feathering (1774). But trying to squeeze all of that into the same matching exercise would not work well. Non-homogeneous responses, for example, are not equally plausible for all premises. Examinees essentially treat them like separate matching exercises anyway.

Another consideration is the weight of matching exercise premises versus MCQs. Were Olivia to use a MCQ here instead of a matching exercise, it might be worth just 1 point, whereas now this issue is worth 3 points. If Olivia is mixing MCQs and matching exercises on an exam, she could simply make MCQs worth 1 point and matching exercise premises worth 1/(# of premises) in the exercise, here 0.33 points. Another alternative is the "Swiss way" (Krebs, 1997), where examinees have to respond to each match correctly to receive 1 point for the entire exercise, or to match two of the three to get partial credit.

The other similar but distinct issue is testing real estate and testing time. Olivia will have to think through the merits of having students respond to one MCQ versus the merits of three premises. Figure 3.2 shows a potential single MCQ about this topic.

Which individual with an interest in events in Boston in 1773 would most likely have thought that the Boston Tea Party was an ill-advised provocation of the British Parliament?

    a) Joyce Junior, an anonymous patriot handbill writer

    b) John Hancock, a Patriot Boston merchant

    c) Benjamin Franklin, agent for Massachusetts in London**

    d) John Adams, Boston lawyer

Figure 3.2 An MCQ on Similar Learning Outcomes to the Matching Exercise

In deciding whether to do the matching exercise or this multiple-choice question, Olivia needs to consider several factors. It will take students less time to respond to the MCQ than to the matching exercise. The MCQ is a smaller sample of the learning objective than the matching exercise is. And, more subtly, while the two measure similar content, how students are expected to know the content is different. In the matching exercise, they really do have to know all of the premises and at least something about each of the responses. In the MCQ, they only need to understand the one premise built into the stem. So Olivia needs to think through these several choices in determining which way is best.

Binary Choice Items

You are no doubt familiar with true/false questions, beloved and bemoaned as they are. They are the best-known example of a broader class of item called the binary choice format or, alternatively, the alternate choice format. Binary choice items present the examinee with a stem and then two options. There is no restriction on what these two options can be, which is where the fun and creativity – and some great learning and assessment – come in. They are often presented in sets, though, with the same two options applying to several stems. In addition to true/false, you could ask fact/opinion, right/wrong, yes/no, or more substantive choices like Patriot/Loyalist, or Federalist/Republican (when Olivia and her students get to the emergence of political parties in the US).

When Jay took the analogous course Olivia is teaching when he was an undergraduate, Professor Smith used binary choice to see if students could distinguish between Federalist and Republican positions on the major political issues of the early nineteenth century. Professor Smith used quotations from primary sources as his stems and "Federalist" and "Republican" as his options. Similarly, it could look like Figure 3.3.

Indicate which political party in the early 1800s was most likely to support each of these issues:		
Strong national (central) government	Federalist**	Republican
Strict interpretation of the constitution	Federalist**	Republican
An agricultural economy	Federalist	Republican**
Cordial relations with France	Federalist	Republican**
Cordial relations with Great Britain	Federalist**	Republican
No national debt	Federalist	Republican**

Figure 3.3 Binary Choice Item with Custom Choices

Which of the following acts of the British Parliament were in direct response to events in Boston and its surroundings? Circle "Yes" if the act was in direct response and "No" if the act was not in direct response.		
Massachusetts Government Act	Yes**	No
Tea Act	Yes	No**
Port Act	Yes**	No
Stamp Act	Yes	No**

Figure 3.4 Binary Choice Item with Yes/No Choices

A variation which is very handy when a MCQ item-writer is in an "All of the above", "None of the above" quandary is multiple true/false (aka Type X items, or check-all-that-apply items). This format consists of a stem with a series of options but the examinee makes a binary response to every option (see Figure 3.4).

The same question written as a check-all-that-apply item, which students essentially treat as multiple true/false questions, would look like Figure 3.5.

There are so many ways to abuse the binary choice format, particularly true/false, that for validity reasons it is important that you follow best practice guidelines. We all remember the "psych"/"double-psych" games instructors have played with us with true/false. The instructor makes them all true, which you don't think she would do, so you change some of your responses to false. Or the popular variant of making the first 10 in a row false. This is a validity issue because student responses indicate how well they picked up on the instructor's pattern and not how well they know the content. And, for us, this goes beyond invalid to unethical. Such patterns are called "response sets". You can avoid response sets among binary choice items by flipping a coin to determine which option the next item will be. Or, if that's impractical given the content, strive to make the responses roughly balanced. You can also write a series of items, about half of each, and then flip the coin to determine whether to put one of the true ones or one of the false ones next.

When writing true/false items, the stems need to be unambiguously true or false. But this leads to true statements tending to be longer than

Which of the following acts of the British Parliament were in direct response to events in Boston and its surroundings? Check all that apply.
☐ Massachusetts Government Act**
☐ Tea Act
☐ Port Act**
☐ Stamp Act

Figure 3.5 Example Check-All-That-Apply Item

false statements, so be careful of stem length within the set. Do not use negative words in true/false stems because students will get turned around inside the possibility of a double negative: a negative statement that is false. Another item-writer phenomenon of unambiguously true statements is that we tend to gravitate toward trivia. Discrete facts are easier to write unambiguously true or false statements about. Yet another issue that comes up with unambiguity is double-barreled stems – that is, stems that have more than one idea in them. Item-writers will sometimes make a true statement false by introducing a second idea: "True or False: The Port Act and the Stamp Act were both passed by the British Parliament in response to events in the Boston area in the 1770s." That's false because the Port Act was but the Stamp Act was not. This is a validity issue because you don't know whether students have any idea what the Port Act was based on their response. Better to use the multiple true/false format, above, to address such an issue.

Other methods of avoiding ambiguity are to use shorter statements; use exact statements; and don't copy text directly from other sources (Jay's Professor Smith used long quotations). One way to add some measurement and validity value is to use student misconceptions as false statements, as we suggested for distractors in MCQs.

Guessing

One of the major issues with supplied response formats which is most acute with binary choice is the ability of the student to guess the answer correctly without knowing it for sure. That is a legitimate concern with supplied response items. There are several ways to address guessing, and we'll talk about some other aspects of that in Chapter 5.

If you are being very clear with your students when they ask, "What will be on the test?", then they should not be too surprised come test day. The less surprised they are, the more likely they'll make an informed choice, even if it's an educated guess. If you're clear with them that you're not playing any games, that you've employed techniques to avoid response sets, then they may be less likely to guess. If you teach them explicit test-taking strategies which will help them to get a clue, they may be less likely to guess.

Context-Dependent Item Sets

One way to get to higher-order thinking and to have tests feel more authentic is to incorporate actual materials like pictures, tables, graphs, large chunks of text (like a newspaper article), software output, screenshots, etc. into the test and ask not one but a series of MCQs about that material. This practice of presenting the examinee with some stimulus and asking a series of MCQs about it has been called an interpretive exercise (e.g. Miller *et al.*, 2012) and

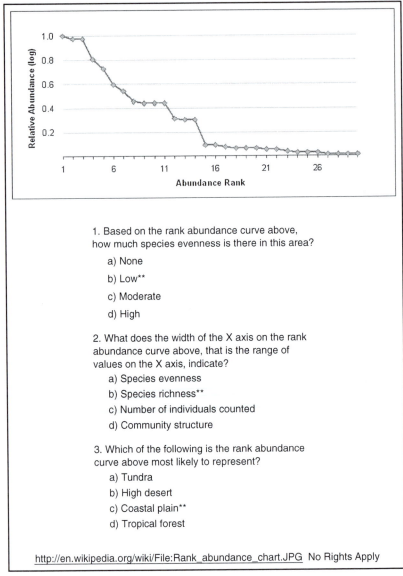

1. Based on the rank abundance curve above,
how much species evenness is there in this area?

   a) None

   b) Low**

   c) Moderate

   d) High

2. What does the width of the X axis on the rank
abundance curve above, that is the range of
values on the X axis, indicate?

   a) Species evenness

   b) Species richness**

   c) Number of individuals counted

   d) Community structure

3. Which of the following is the rank abundance
curve above most likely to represent?

   a) Tundra

   b) High desert

   c) Coastal plain**

   d) Tropical forest

http://en.wikipedia.org/wiki/File:Rank_abundance_chart.JPG No Rights Apply

Figure 3.6 Example Context-Dependent Item Set

a context-dependent item set (Haladyna, 1992). Figure 3.6 shows a possible
example from Sam Oliver's course.

This format has a great deal of flexibility and potential. Having the
stimulus material can spark your item-writing. We find it easier to write

items around a stimulus than to write each one from scratch. This format also permits more authenticity to enter into your tests. You can be asking questions about "real" things such as software output or actual artwork, for example. Doing so also helps you and your students contextualize the knowledge rather than seeing their knowledge in discrete little bits. Even a factual, knowledge-level item in this context shows how knowing that fact relates to other issues.

This format brings with it some particular best practice guidelines. One of the downsides to the connection of items to a stimulus is that then the items are connected with each other. So you need to take particular care not to cue examinees; that is, not to give away the answer to one question in another question. This can be more challenging than it sounds. Another downside of the connection is that if an examinee somehow misunderstands the stimulus, it could mean they miss several items, not just one. So you want to be careful in your choice of stimulus. It increases the higher-order thinking if you pick a stimulus that students haven't seen before, but that novelty could also mean they don't recognize the concepts you've been working with in class.

Vignette-Based MCQs

A popular technique for introducing some authenticity, but in a single MCQ, is the vignette-based MCQ. Here, the stem presents a vignette or scenario which ends in a question. These are currently widely used in medical education and licensure testing as well as in other healthcare professions. The most important aspect of authenticity in a vignette is not the details and the reality of it, rather that it puts the examinee into a scenario for which your course is preparing them and requires the same kind of thinking of them. Focusing on the degree to which the vignette sounds like the "real world" makes you susceptible to the issues of window dressing discussed in the previous chapter. But focusing on the degree to which the examinee needs to think through a real-world issue relevant to your course and learning objectives improves the validity of your assessment.

One of the key learning objectives in Sam Oliver's ecology class is understanding the different methodologies for conducting a census of species in a particular area. Students need to know the basics about the species being targeted, what sampling techniques are viable, what study designs are appropriate, etc. This lends itself well to vignette-based MCQs. Look at the two items in Figure 3.7.

Both items are working with the fit of a particular population abundance study design to a set of circumstances. The first item, though, requires only memorization. The second item requires first that examinees extract the relevant information from the vignette and then match that information to the parameters necessary for the listed study designs.

Which of the following approaches to determining the population of a numerous species that is not highly mobile and/or that resides in an enclosed area would provide the most accurate result?

   a) true census

   b) mark-recapture design**

   c) plot sampling

   d) distance sampling

The New Mexico Department of Game and Fish wishes to determine if it is time to restock tiger muskellunge (*Esox masquinongy x Esox lucius*) in Bluewater Lake (surface area of 1,200 acres). They have determined that the population should be about 7,000 of this species. Which of the following approaches to determining the number of tiger muskies in the lake would best suit this circumstance?

   a) true census

   b) mark-recapture design**

   c) plot sampling

   d) distance sampling

Figure 3.7 Example Vignette-Based MCQs

This second item also mimics a question that a staff biologist would actually have to address.

Complex Multiple-Choice (Type K) Items

The last variation we want to explore is called complex multiple-choice, or Type K, items. (Other aliases include multiple completion, and multiple multiple-choice (Albanese, 1993).) We are presenting this format because, even though its use is rising again, it has been roundly discredited through research. So, unlike the other formats we've discussed in this chapter, we recommend *against* the use of this one.

Among the motivations for this format is that much of the content we want students to learn doesn't boil down to a single, correct answer. It's more complicated than that. Type K permits some version of "choose all that apply" while still resulting in a single response. This format was born at the Educational Testing Service and was also used by the National Board of Medical Examiners for this reason (Albanese, 1993; Haladyna, 1992). It is an attempt to provide a form which can capture some complexity. Figure 3.8 shows an example, potentially from Sam Oliver's General Ecology course, to get us going.

In a Type K item, the stem is followed by a series of primary responses, any combination of which could be correct. Then the secondary options are combinations of primary responses from which the examinee must choose. While the goal of getting at concepts where there is more than one answer

Which of these factors are hypothesized to explain why there are more species near the equator than toward the poles?

I. Glaciation affected the temperate regions.
II. The tropics have more light, water, and nutrients.
III. Solar winds affect the tropics more.
IV. The temperate regions have less diversity of species.
V. The tropics are warmer.

a) I, II, and III
b) I, II, III, IV
c) I, III, V
d) I, II, IV, V**

Figure 3.8 Example Complex Multiple-Choice (Type K) Item

is important, this is the wrong approach for several reasons. Such items take up a lot of temporal and spatial real estate on the exam itself. From a validity perspective, "testwiseness" (rather than content knowledge) can change an examinee's chances of guessing, because if any of the responses can be eliminated, potentially multiple options containing that response can also be eliminated (cf. Albanese, 1993). Another validity issue is that since the options only present a subset of all possible combinations of responses to the examinee as potentially correct, a study of those options can clue an examinee to one or more right responses (Albanese, 1993). Put more plainly, the item itself might be giving clues about the right or wrong answers to the examinees. In the example, response I appears in all four options, so a test-wise student would not even read that first response; it's automatically in. From a cognitive load perspective, this format is very taxing. Examinees first need to comprehend the stem. Then they need to evaluate the responses. Then they need to match the options to those responses. This is very time-consuming for examinees. And, related to these effects, such items tend not to have high technical qualities, so they tend not to contribute to good measurement and may be dropped from further use inside of a testing program (Haladyna, 1992).

If examinees need to evaluate each of the responses in order to navigate a Type K item, why not make that the main activity? In other words, why not make the item a multiple true/false where the examinees responds "true" or "false" to each of the responses, as we've already discussed?

Summary

These variations and elaborations provide much flexibility and many options to you as an assessor. Watch for ways in your own testing to work with some or all of these formats!

References and Resources for Further Reading

Albanese, M. (1993). Type K and other complex multiple-choice items: An analysis of research and item properties. *Educational Measurement: Issues and Practice*, 12(1), 28–33.

Haladyna, T. M. (1992). The effectiveness of several multiple choice formats. *Applied Measurement in Education*, 5(1), 73–88.

Krebs, R. (1997). The Swiss way to score multiple true-false items: Theoretical and empirical evidence. In A. Scherpbier, C. van der Vleuten, J. Rethans, and A. van der Steeg (eds.) *Advances in Medical Education* (158–61). Dordrecht: Kluwer.

Miller, M. D., Linn, R. L., and Gronlund, N. E. (2012). *Measurement and Assessment in Teaching* (11th ed.). New York: Pearson.

Section II

Assessing with Multiple-Choice Questions

4 Test Blueprints

We like instructional tools that provide a lot of bang for the buck, that serve as levers which lift more weight than the force applied to them. Test blueprints can be very powerful levers whose impacts affect your test planning and writing; the alignment between your instructional activities and your assessments; and your students' learning. All in one table!

"What'll Be on the Test?"

We're willing to bet it hasn't been that long since a student asked you: "What'll be on the test?" (This is a little different from the question, "Will that [specific bit of information] be on the test?" Jay jokes that he is only ever asked this question once per semester because his response is, "You know, I hadn't thought of that, what a good idea!"). While the student who asked you probably isn't conscious of it, she is actually asking you for three different pieces of information: *What* will be on the test? (content); *How* will it be on the test? (ways of knowing); and *How much of it* will be on the test? (proportions). These are questions to which you really must have good solid answers for yourself, because they are identical to the questions, "What will you teach in the class?", "How will you teach it?", and "How much instructional time, space, and energy will you and your students invest in it?" You cannot teach well, let alone assess well, if you don't have good, solid answers to these questions.

What Will Be on the Test?

Test – and course – content is perhaps the easiest for us to think about. There is usually a textbook, divided into chapters, which serves as a source of and organization for content. You also likely have learning objectives, sometimes referred to as student learning outcomes, which articulate what students should be able to do or know by the end of your course. For the purposes of this book, we use learning objectives to refer to the measurable and observable skills, knowledge, or attributes you want your students to have at the end of an instructional unit or course. The important part of a learning objective is that the focus is on what you want your students to learn. (For a discussion on how to write student learning objectives/outcomes, see Gronlund and Brookhart, 2009.) Perhaps the degree program in which you teach has sets of core knowledge or competencies which all students are to master, some of which are to be primarily addressed through your course. It is possible that your course content draws on statements from professional organizations or licensing bodies about what students in a given field should know and be able to do. You've also got your own syllabus which hopefully synthesizes all of these for students and perhaps distills them into a course agenda articulating what content will be addressed during what class meetings and other experiences. So, the question, "What will be on the test?" is perhaps the easiest one to respond to.

Professor Sam Oliver's ecology course has an entire section devoted to population growth and the impact of other species on a species' rise or fall. While there are no industry definitions of what should be in such an ecology course at college specifically, studying populations is required to be a Certified Ecologist (www.esa.org/esa/careers-and-certification/certification/) by the Ecological Society of America, and such knowledge is inherent in the Competency Framework of the Chartered Institute of Ecology and Environmental Management in order to become a Chartered Ecologist (www.cieem.net/further-details-eligibility). Sam also draws on his own expertise in the area to determine that these topics are critical content. He is confirmed in this because all the major textbooks appropriate for this course include several chapters about these issues. Therefore, at the course level, on the syllabus, he has this major student learning objective: "Students will be able to explain and analyze the factors that impact population growth and decline." Given the size of that topic in the course, Sam could devote an entire exam to those topics. This learning objective breaks down into subcomponents:

1   Students will be able to define and analyze the impacts of predation on population growth and decline.
2   Students will be able to define and analyze the impacts of parasitism and infectious diseases on population growth and decline.
3   Students will be able to define and analyze the impacts of competition on population growth and decline.

Those topics are "What will be on Sam's test".

How Will it Be on the Test?

The answers to this question are perhaps more important than the "What" question, to you and to your students; however, you're much less likely to have an explicit answer to this question. There are two different prongs to these answers: "What will it look like on the test?" and "In what ways do you expect students to know the content?"

The format of the exam is the more immediate and concrete answer to this question. What kinds of test questions will be on the test? In this book, we're focused on multiple-choice questions. And there are other formats you can include in addition to MCQs on an exam: fill-in-the-blank, short essay, etc. So one way to respond to "How will the content be on the test?" is to articulate what item types you will use on the test itself. Sam is going to use traditional MCQs and a couple of short essay questions.

The second prong to your answer is, "In what ways do you expect students to know the content?" When considering your expectations for your students, you have in mind what you want them to know, but that probably includes some sense of how you want them to know it. Let's suppose that you want students to know the formula associated with Newton's second law of motion, $F = ma$, where F is force; m is mass; and a is acceleration. How do you want students to know this? Will you expect them to have the formula memorized, or will it be provided to them? Do you expect them to label the terms? Do you expect to hand them some data and have them calculate the terms? Must they apply the formula to a scenario to solve a problem? Must they see a scenario and know that this formula, and not some other, is most applicable? Do you expect them to justify lower speed limits on congested roads as a matter of public safety policy based on the relationships inherent in the formula? Do you want students to have read the *Principia* themselves and discuss how Newton's original Latin phrasing of this Law has been translated and mistranslated over the years? Do you expect students to be able to articulate the bounds of this Law, such as how the Lorentz factor needs to be applied under special relativity? Do you want students to be able to articulate how this expression fits into the larger philosophies of the enlightenment?

Hopefully, our questions have proven a couple of points. First, you *do* think, at least implicitly, about how you want students to know content. Second, it is critical that you do, because you won't know how or what to teach without having done so. We explored numerous possibilities, too many to address in any single course, we suspect, around a small, three-term formula. Now consider a central, big idea in your field, in one of your courses. No, really, we'll wait. Have one in mind? Run through that little thought exercise we just did with $F = ma$.

Some of the options you generated came quickly to you out of your innate sense of what aspects of that big idea are appropriate for lower division courses, upper division courses, or graduate courses. And you also considered your students, too: what they can handle, and why they need to know it one way before they can tackle it in another way or deepen their knowledge.

Perhaps it would prove useful for completing this exercise if you had some frameworks or taxonomies for articulating different *Ways of Knowing*.

Ways of Knowing is our generic, broad term for the variety of extant frameworks available to you for articulating different cognitive, affective, behavioral, and physical levels in which students engage content. It turns out there are many frameworks to choose from.

The exemplar of Ways of Knowing is Bloom's Taxonomy, of which most people have heard. The team Benjamin Bloom headed articulated a six-level taxonomy of cognitive learning objectives in 1956. (Actually, Bloom's team wrote cognitive, affective, and psychomotor taxonomies, the latter two of which are far less well known. And it was a team, a committee actually, and authorship on the different taxonomies rotated. Bloom's happened to be the first name on the cognitive taxonomy. David Krathwohl was first author on the affective domain publication, which is still used but much less well known. Krathwohl has recently participated in producing a revised cognitive taxonomy (Anderson *et al.*, 2001).) The original cognitive taxonomy included these levels: knowledge, understanding, application, analysis, synthesis and evaluation. The new taxonomy is: remembering, understanding, applying, analyzing, evaluating, and creating. To quickly illustrate these, we've aligned our earlier questions about $F = ma$ with those levels in Table 4.1.

While we do not wish to minimize important distinctions between the original and the revised versions and to assume perfect commensurability between terms, for reasons we're about to explain, we did offer a pretty high-level gloss of these levels in the table.

Bloom's is the best-known and best-resourced cognitive taxonomy (see http://larryferlazzo.edublogs.org/2009/05/25/the-best-resources-for-helping-teachers-use-blooms-taxonomy-in-the-classroom/ for a dizzying array of articulations and resources about this taxonomy). But there are many, many others. As we've mentioned, Bloom's committee actually produced three different sets. And, since that original work, many other taxonomies have been developed and are offered for your use.

One of the implications of so many taxonomies is that none of them is "right" or "true". They each take a different approach to articulating various Ways of Knowing. It's not important that you pick the "true" taxonomy for you and your students; rather, it's important that you pick a taxonomy that will aid you and your students in articulating how you expect them to know the material. One of the simplest ones we've encountered shows up in professional schools like medicine and law: Knows That, Knows How, Shows How, and Can Do (Miller, 1990). Take a few minutes with this very elegant taxonomy and return to your big idea you worked with earlier. How would you articulate that idea through this taxonomy?

For Sam's students, Knows That would include knowledge of the concepts of predation, infectious diseases, parasitism and competition. Knows How might include explaining how each of those concepts relates to population growth and decline in the generic or abstract sense. Shows How could include articulating why jackrabbits became so scarce in a certain county.

Table 4.1 Example Questions Aligned to Bloom's Original and Revised Taxonomies

Bloom's Original	Blooms Revised	F = ma	Predation in Sam's course
Knowledge	Remembering	Will you expect them to have the formula memorized?	Will they have to define predation?
Understanding	Understanding	Do you expect them to label the terms?	Will students need to explain how coyotes are predators?
Application	Applying	Do you expect them to justify lower speed limits on congested roads as a matter of public safety policy based on the relationships inherent in the formula?	If a coyote pack moves out of an area, what impact will that have on the jackrabbit population?
Analysis	Analyzing	Do you want students to have read the *Principia* themselves and discuss how Newton's original Latin phrasing of this Law has been translated and mistranslated over the years?	Will Sam expect students to distinguish between predation, detritivory, and scavenging?
Synthesis	Creating	Do you want students to be able to articulate how this expression fits into the larger philosophies of the enlightenment?	Will Sam ask students to write an environmental impact plan on other species of introducing coyote to an area where there have been none?
Evaluation	Evaluating	Do you expect students to be able to articulate the bounds of this Law, such as how the Lorentz factor needs to be applied under special relativity?	Sam could ask his students to write a critique of federal reintroduction plans such as ones for bison or Mexican wolves with a specific emphasis on predation.

And Can Do could be writing a plan for the successful reintroduction of a species back into a state park.

Find some taxonomies; do some asking around among colleagues; and select a taxonomy which will help you and your students be more articulate about how you want them to know the content. You can even create your own or modify existing ones, as long as it makes sense to you and your students (and to your colleagues – a little external validation is a good thing).

How Much of It Will Be on the Test?

As you look at your syllabus for your course, you've got learning objectives listed there, perhaps many of them. Let's say you've got ten learning objectives for your course. Is each learning objective equally important? We doubt it. Sam has seven major learning objectives, including the one above. Perhaps the first exam in your course is going to cover the first four weeks of the class wherein you covered the first four chapters of the textbook, one per week. We doubt that, too. In Sam's case, populations get introduced in one section, but then make up the next section of three weeks entirely. So you and Sam have already done some prioritizing of content. You've done some of this thinking when you wrote the agenda portion of your course syllabus: what topics you intend to cover on which dates. So you're spending the first two weeks on chapter 1 because it's so foundational and then a week on chapter 2 and then chapters 3 and 4 during the fourth week, which are applications. Perhaps you inherited a course, share a course, or otherwise need to implement decisions which others have made about what content happens when. If the chunks of content are not evenly distributed across time blocks, chances are you've got a good reason for that. Perhaps you know from experience that one concept is much more difficult for students to grasp than others so it gets more class time, or its own homework assignment. Perhaps some content is much more important in your field than other content so it receives more attention. In Sam's case, population growth and decline is one of the core, fundamental issues in the entire field. Those same considerations which have driven your allocation of class time and other resources like assignments, practice problems, lab time, etc. are also relevant to allocating testing time and resources like multiple-choice questions. If, to go back to the simple example, you're going to spend 25 percent of instructional time and resources on each one of four chapters, then 25 percent of the testing real estate should also be devoted to each chapter: say, 12–13 MCQs on a 50-item test.

So when that student inevitably asks you, "What'll be on the test?", you've got some very articulate thinking behind your answer. Wouldn't a tool for capturing, systematizing, perhaps even automating this thinking and these decisions be great? Some of this work is being done by your course syllabus, although it likely doesn't make the articulation sufficiently clear with respect to the test itself. For that, you need a test blueprint.

Your Test Blueprint Pulls It All Together

A test blueprint is a table with two or three dimensions in it. The first dimension, usually in the rows, is the taxonometric articulation of Ways of Knowing. The second dimension, usually in the columns, is the different Content areas. The third dimension, often represented as a second-level division of rows, is item types, if there are more than one type. The cells in

Table 4.2 Generic Example of a Test Blueprint

		Chapter 1	Chapter 2	Chapter 3	Chapter 4	
True/False	Knows That	6 (12%)	3 (6%)	1 (2%)	0	10 (20%)
MCQ	Knows That	4 (8%)	2 (4%)	1 (2%)	2 (4%)	
	Knows How	10 (20%)	2 (4%)	7 (14%)	6 (12%)	34 (68%)
Short Essay	Shows How	0	1 (2%)	3 (6%)	2 (4%)	6 (12%) 50 (100%)
Totals	Knows That	10 (20%)	5 (10%)	2 (4%)	2 (4%)	19 (58%)
	Knows How	10 (20%)	2 (4%)	7 (14%)	6 (12%)	25 (30%)
	Shows How	0	1 (2%)	3 (6%)	2 (4%)	6 (12%)
		20 (40%)	8 (16%)	12 (24%)	10 (20%)	50 (100%)

the table, then, contain the proportion of testing real estate allocated to that combination of Ways of Knowing and Content. The cells can contain the actual number of items (better for you when item-writing) or the percentage of total items (better for students as a study guide). Table 4.2 shows a generic example; Table 4.3 illustrates how Sam's might look.

Let's consider Sam's blueprint carefully. As a reminder, here are Sam's three learning objectives: 1) Students will be able to define and analyze the impacts of predation on population growth and decline. 2) Students will be able to define and analyze the impacts of parasitism and infectious diseases on population growth and decline. 3) Students will be able to define and analyze the impacts of competition on population growth and decline.

Notice first that the main content idea (e.g. predation) from the learning objectives becomes the column in the blueprint. Notice next that the

Table 4.3 Example Test Blueprint for a Biology Course

		Predation	Parasitism and infectious diseases	Competition	
MCQ	Define	4 (8%)	2 (4%)	4 (8%)	10 (20%)
	Explain	8 (16%)	8 (16%)	9 (18%)	25 (50%)
	Analyze	2 (4%)	4 (8%)	5 (10%)	11 (22%)
Short essay	Analyze	1 (2%)	1 (2%)	2 (2%)	4 (8%) 50 (100%)
Totals	Define	4 (8%)	2 (4%)	4 (8%)	10 (20%)
	Explain	8 (16%)	8 (16%)	9 (18%)	25 (50%)
	Analyze	3 (6%)	5 (10%)	7 (14%)	15 (30%)
		15 (30%)	15 (30%)	20 (40%)	50 (100%)

verb(s) in the learning objectives become the rows. When Sam built his table, he began with the bottom, or summary portion. He asked himself, how did the three different topics need to be apportioned? Based on the many considerations we outlined earlier, he decided on a 30-30-40 division. Then he asked himself how the Ways of Knowing should be divided. Here he took his own philosophy of the content into account, how the textbook presents the material, how he organizes in-class and out-of-class experiences, etc., and he determined that definition could not be dismissed but wasn't as important as explanation and analysis, and that analysis, in this introductory course on the topic, wasn't yet as important as explanation. So he apportioned them with explanation weighing more than analysis and analysis weighing more than definition. With those proportions set, completing the cells becomes a bit of a mathematical exercise: the proportion of the row times the proportion of the column gives the proportion of items that should be in a particular cell (e.g. 20 percent definition x 40 percent competition = 8 percent should be definition items about competition). That translates into four items in that cell. It doesn't have to be exact, for example, due to rounding.

It's also possible to weight items differently. For example, on short quizzes, the math may not align well to individual questions. That is, on a 10-item quiz, each item scored equally is worth 10 percent, but suppose you judge that some of them should be worth 5 percent. You can weight the items differently – not all have equal weight – when you calculate the score.

How many rows and columns should you have? What level of particularity should be captured in the content dimension? Is there a right taxonomy? It is possible to get very technologically sophisticated with this construction (e.g. Gabli *et al.*, 2013). It's also possible to get caught up in constructing your blueprint, make it an end in itself, and lose some of its value. Susan Brookhart (1999) articulates that your blueprint should be reasonably quick and easy for you to construct and work with; that too many cells probably signals an overspecification of content; and that, essentially, it's possible to make complete precision and articulation the enemy of a meaningful and useful tool for you and your students. In the same way that you've already been making proportion decisions about content when you wrote the schedule for the syllabus, let this be somewhat rough-cut, too. In your syllabus, you don't have your schedule mapped out to the minute (we hope!). In that same spirit, you don't need to have the proportions here mapped out to a single digit, let alone to a decimal place!

If getting a blueprint started remains daunting, try pulling out an old exam from a previous semester and construct the post-hoc blueprint from it. How does that post-hoc blueprint match your current intentions?

It is worth noting that, among educational measurement experts, there are two different types of these tables. Historically and most formally, a "test blueprint" had just one dimension to it, the content areas with proportions, while a "table of specifications", or sometimes "test specifications", added the taxonomy dimension (Bridge *et al.*, 2003). We, and many others, often refer to the latter also as a test blueprint. That is, the two terms get conflated. In this book, we prefer the term test blueprint to refer to a table of specifications because it's intuitively evocative of the concept of a plan for the test itself.

This one table distills numerous instructional and assessment decisions into one location and makes it really easy to plan your instruction, align your instruction and assessment, plan your assessment, and confirm that what you want to do, need to do, and are doing, are coherent or *aligned*. It becomes a critical document for you and your students before instruction, during instruction, and after instruction as well as before you test them.

Using the Blueprint Before You Teach and They Learn

We recommend that you create a test blueprint *before* you begin teaching these four chapters, perhaps yet without the item types and numbers of items (i.e. the "Totals" section of the table). We've already made the point that you need to be making the decisions about how to apportion your instructional time with respect to the four chapters. Now it's evident in the table that you also need to consider how you and your students will spend the chapter 1 time. Given that the chapter 1 column is equally split between Knows That and Knows How, your instructional activities should also support that even split, for example.

Sam will be emphasizing explanation in all that he does. It's important to note that, before constructing the test blueprint, Sam wasn't as clear that explanation was so important to him or that analysis, in his mind, would come later for these students. But now that he has that clarity, it will permeate his instruction.

If you as the instructor need to know which content is more important and which is less important, how you want students to know the content, and how those two come together for instruction and assessment, *so do your students*.

While You're Teaching and They're Learning

Another reason we suggest you write the blueprint before you teach is so you can give it to your students. You should encourage, and perhaps even teach, your students how to use the blueprint to focus their study time as well as their study approaches. Should they be memorizing using flashcards, should they be developing their own examples, etc.? This is not pure "test prep" or "study skills" instruction, which many instructors see as "not their job". You can couch these lessons as ways of communicating how practitioners in your field view the importance of content and how they use the content. Why you've chosen to spend two weeks on chapter 1 and have it be 40 percent of the test would be important things for your students to know, as would examples of how the knowledge is applied in the field.

As Sam starts this section of the course about population growth, he gives this blueprint to students and discusses with them explicitly why population growth is so important, why it's worth this much time and attention, and why explanation is so important at this stage in their learning. It absolutely changes the "What will be on the test?" dynamic for Sam and his students. Sam essentially heads off the question by proactively addressing those issues while they are mostly about the content and the students' learning of the content, rather than about the test and the score.

There is also opportunity to use the blueprint in class. At the end of each week, you could briefly refer to the blueprint as a class and ask if the proportions are still accurate. We've all had the experience of spending additional time on a topic than we originally intended, either through their learning needs or even our own zeal. Whether the blueprint should be adjusted is something you could gain student input on.

The test blueprint should form a map of student study time. Just as it apportions test real estate and instructional time, it should also apportion their study time and activities. The Ways of Knowing dimension should guide them to appropriate study activities. A little class time here on your part, particularly with less experienced students, would be well spent. Help them to see how to translate the blueprint into study activities.

One of the most common sources of student complaints about assessment is that it doesn't match what happened in class or what was in the readings, and while students may have trouble articulating it, often the mismatch is with proportion. Now, though, you and your students have explicitly kept track of these proportions by tweaking a blueprint together.

With the basic blueprint in hand, you now can take a look at what item types you'd like to use, and how much testing time you have; and make some decisions about how many items and of what kind to use. We've spent an entire section of this book on item-writing, so here we'll simply comment that once you and your students have finalized the blueprint so it matches instruction, you can use it to write test items.

As you write the test, the blueprint will shape your natural item-writing tendencies. The research on writing test questions shows that if item-writers are not guided by a blueprint they will write items at lower taxonomic levels and on topics they know or like better. Suppose chapter 3 is your favorite. Left to your own devices, you'll write more chapter 3 questions than are warranted. By writing items with your blueprint in front of you, you'll check those natural proclivities and write a more balanced test.

This is the rationale for developing the test blueprint from the outside in rather than from the inside out; that is, from the rows and columns (the marginal) toward the cells and not from the cells to the marginal. To write a test without a blueprint is to start in some cell and let the test grow. That will produce a very different set of proportions on the rows and columns and likely ones that aren't what you would intend.

A Final Benefit

Test blueprints also serve a more technical purpose. Psychometrics – the science of testing – defines some key elements of testing quality, and primary among them is validity. Validity is the degree to which you can show evidence to support your claims about what your test is measuring. While test validity can be an extremely involved and technical topic, for you, your students, and other stakeholders in your students' learning, it is very straightforward. Whether you explicitly acknowledge it or not, you are making a validity argument that the results of your classroom test indicate the degree of mastery your students have of the learning objectives it addresses. Constructing and using a test blueprint as we have described it provides very strong evidence of how the test you administered matched the teaching and learning intended.

Summary

A test blueprint is a powerful alignment tool that keeps your instruction, your students' studying, your assessment design, and your assessment aligned. It can also serve as evidence of the quality of your test.

References and Resources for Further Reading

Anderson, L., Krathwohl, D., Airasian, P., Cruikshank, K., Mayer, R., Pintrich, P., Raths, J. and Wittrock, M. (2001). *A Revision of Bloom's Taxonomy of Educational Objectives*. New York, NY: Pearson.

Bloom, B. S. and Krathwohl, D. R. (1956) Taxonomy of educational objectives: The classification of educational goals, by a committee of college and university examiners. *Handbook 1: Cognitive domain*. New York, NY, Longmans.

Bridge, P. D., Musial, J., Frank, R., Roe, T., and Sawilowsky, S. (2003). Measurement practices: Methods for developing content-valid student examinations. *Medical Teacher*, 25(4), 414–21.

Brookhart, S. M. (1999). The art and science of classroom assessment: The missing part of pedagogy. *ASHE-ERIC Higher Education Research Reports*, 27(1), 1–102.

Cantrell, P. (2012). Using test blueprints to measure student learning in middle school science classrooms. *The Researcher*, 24(1), 55–71.

Fives, H. and DiDonato-Barnes, N. (2013). Classroom test construction: The power of a table of specifications. *Practical Assessment, Research & Evaluation*, 18(3).

Gabli, M., Jaara, E. M., and Mermri, E. B. (2013). A technological tool to optimize educational assessment. *iJET*, 8(6), 62–5.

Gronlund, N. E. and Brookhart, S. M. (2009). *Gronlund's Writing Instructional Objectives*. Upper Saddle River, NJ: Pearson/Merrill Prentice Hall.

Guskey, T. R. (2005). Mapping the road to proficiency. *Educational Leadership*, 63(3), 32–8.

Miller, G. E. (1990). The assessment of clinical skills/competence/performance. *Academic Medicine*, 65(9), S63–S67.

Notar, C. E., Zuelke, D. C., Wilson, J. D., and Yunker, B. D. (2004). The table of specifications: Insuring accountability in teacher made tests. *Journal of Instructional Psychology*, 31(2), 115–29.

Marzano, R. J. and Pickering, D. J. (1997). *Dimensions of Learning Teacher's Manual* (2nd ed.). Alexandria, VA: ASCD.

5 Test Construction, Administration, and Scoring

Now that you understand the basics of creating a multiple-choice question and how to create variations based on those foundational principles, you need to consider how to bring all the pieces together to create a quiz, test, or other assessment. An assessment is more than a collection of questions, even ones carefully crafted according to a blueprint. Well before your students see the assessment, you'll need to determine how best to assemble your MCQs, what administration details need to be included, and how you intend to score the questions.

Test Construction

An important, but often overlooked, component of creating a multiple-choice assessment is putting all the questions together to create a coherent assessment. Does the order of the questions matter? Should they be organized by difficulty, topic, or some other feature? Should there be more than one form? This chapter will explore best practices in constructing a multiple-choice assessment which assesses the concepts instructors are trying to measure without introducing extraneous factors.

When we discussed item-writing earlier in the book, we used a framework of validity concerns and cognitive load concerns to organize the best practice guidelines. That framework works very well for how to put your tests together, too. A poorly constructed assessment may introduce what is known as construct-irrelevant variance, also known as construct contamination, a validity concern. This occurs when test scores are systematically influenced by factors not part of the "construct" being assessed. For example, including questions on a test that contain vocabulary unrelated to the content may unduly influence a student's score. Additionally, including contexts or situations that are potentially offensive to some test-takers – without a measurement purpose – should be avoided (AERA *et al.*, 2014). If your student learning objectives are related to issues that some students may find offensive, but they're legitimate, those are totally relevant to your course and should be on the test.

In addition to considering issues related to construct-irrelevant variance, you should also be aware of how your test construction impacts a student's cognitive load. Are your students thinking mostly about the test content during the test and minimally about the test-taking process, or are they spending considerable time navigating the test itself? Cognitive load theory recommends that a task should avoid elements that will overload students' ability to process the task on which they are working. While the specific elements of your MCQ could influence cognitive load, so can the way in which the entire assessment is constructed. Miller (2011) found that improving the organization and flow of questions in an assessment administered via computer reduced cognitive load for test-takers. To reduce cognitive load, you should remove elements of an assessment that might disproportionately influence a student's cognitive load (Sweller, 1994).

When constructing your assessment, paying attention to validity considerations and cognitive load allows your students to think about the content, not how to navigate the test. Let's look at some strategies for minimizing construct-irrelevant variance and cognitive load. These sound like really simple things but that's where their power to impact student learning resides. Numbering pages (if administering a paper-and-pencil test) or displaying a progress bar (if computer-administered) actually works in several ways. Numbering the pages (and the MCQs themselves) can prevent students from inadvertently skipping pages. And if you number "Page 3 of 12", the page numbers serve as a progress bar, which helps students manage their test-taking time.

How the questions actually appear on the page matters. List questions in a single column rather than a double column to avoid crowding questions on a page. Double columns of items are difficult for students to navigate. Even when the items are numbered, students will get confused and some will move through the test in rows and others in columns, which, of course, causes them to misplace their answers on your scoring sheet.

Have diagrams and tables *above* the question using the information, *not* below. If you're using context-dependent item sets or large diagrams or tables, consider presenting them on a separate sheet outside of the test booklet so that students can put the diagram next to the test booklet. Both the stimulus material (e.g. a table or diagram) and the items in the test booklet should be explicitly linked. For example, if you're doing a context-dependent item set of six items all about a graph, then write a separate set of directions before that first item which states this, e.g., "The next six items, numbers 40–45, all refer to Figure 2 on the attached sheets." Then in the attached sheets, at Figure 2, the directions will say, "The graph in Figure 2 is to be used to respond to items 40 through 45 in the test booklet." See Figure 5.1 for an example of how to format a page using these guidelines.

Results are mixed in terms of research on the effects of question order and test performance. Covington and Omelich (1987) and Carlson and Ostrosky

---

Page 1 of 2

Question 1: A group of 100 students is given an IQ test and the distribution has a mean of 100 and a standard deviation of 15. If every student's IQ score is divided by 5, what would be the standard deviation of the distribution?

A) 3**
B) 5
C) 9
D) 10
E) 15

Question 2: An instructor conducted an item analysis on her 10-question quiz. She obtained the following results:

Item Analysis (10 questions) – correct answer is in **bold**

ITEM	P-value	Discrimination value	A	B	C	D	E
1.	0.68	0.35	30	187	37	**566**	11
2.	0.89	0.20	**739**	5	1	9	77
3.	0.55	0.37	4	233	46	88	**460**
4.	0.99	-0.05	**822**	3	3	3	0
5.	0.93	0.13	24	0	12	**775**	20
6.	0.74	-0.02	25	16	**615**	35	140
7.	0.40	0.33	68	107	**334**	165	157
8.	0.26	0.09	114	168	**213**	160	176
9.	0.14	0.03	75	64	**120**	67	505
10.	0.46	0.45	**379**	98	74	83	197

On which item did the highest proportion of students correctly answer the question?

A. Item 1
B. Item 4**
C. Item 6
D. Item 9
E. Item 10

Continue on to page 2

Figure 5.1 Example Format for an MCQ Assessment

(1992) found that when a test is initially perceived as easy students will have less test anxiety. These findings suggest that easier items should be placed at the beginning of a test and harder questions at the end. Gohmann and Spector (1989) did not find any effects of item order on test anxiety. Newman, Kundert, Lane, and Sather Bull (1988) found that the order of MCQs based on statistical item difficulty had no impact on overall test score. However, they found that students scored higher on hard items when questions were ordered in increasing cognitive difficulty as measured by Bloom's taxonomy, regardless of the statistical difficulty order. Leary and Dorans (1985) conducted a review of literature on the effects of item order in alternative forms that contain the same set of questions. They found that in general, student performance did not differ in the easy-to-hard arrangement of questions compared to a random-order arrangement when students were given ample time to complete the assessment (a power test rather than a speeded test).

Gronlund (1988) recommends ordering the questions by content, by item format, and then by increasing difficulty of items. This rule is based on information processing principles, making it a cognitive load consideration. It is easier mentally for students to answer all of the items about one content before moving on to another. They also perform similar mental tasks on similar items before changing mental tasks with other formats. Finally, putting easy items before hard items helps students gain some success early on.

Research by Huntley and Welch (1993) found that item difficulty did not vary when distractors on a mathematics assessment were placed in a logical (ascending or descending) order compared to a random order, but that discrimination values were higher for questions with randomly ordered distractors. They concluded that randomly ordering options may pose challenges for low ability students. In general, options should be ordered logically or numerically, as we previously recommended in Chapter 2.

Creating Alternate Forms

Given the recommendations above for how best to assemble your multiple-choice questions into a coherent whole, what implications do they have for creating alternate forms of a paper assessment or scrambling the order of questions and/or answer choices in an online assessment? If you use item banks to create *parallel* forms which have different sets of questions intended to assess the same learning objectives, the test should have the same number of questions, the questions should be the same difficulty, and the instructions, time limits, and formats should be the same. Note that it can be challenging to construct MCQ assessments that match these guidelines. If you create *alternate* forms, which have the same set of questions but in a different order, the best strategy is to create a random order for all versions of the assessment so that one is not "easy-to-hard" and the other is random.

Using the strategies described above for organizing your MCQs into a coherent assessment helps reduce the chances of introducing construct-irrelevant variance and the cognitive load placed on your students while completing the assessment.

Test Administration

In addition to the quality of the MCQs included on an assessment, the conditions under which a multiple-choice assessment is administered can influence student performance. Knowing how to frame the instructions, how much time to allot per question, and whether to administer the test in a classroom or online, are all important considerations to decide as a part of the test administration process.

First, provide complete instructions as to how the assessment is to be taken. This has both validity and cognitive load implications. If students don't understand *how* they are supposed to take the test, it will influence what the score means. There is such a thing as testwiseness, but you really don't want it having a negative impact on students' scores. Good directions also have a cognitive load element because they reduce the amount of cognitive effort students have to expend to figure out how to take the test. They can spend their thinking on the content, not the process of test-taking. Specifically, identify the number of points for each question or section on the assessment. Letting students know the relative importance of each question helps them to allocate their efforts. If you are using a variety of MCQ formats, you may wish to write separate directions for each section.

Additionally, provide recommendations to students about how much time to spend on each question or section. To determine how much time to allocate, practice taking the completed test yourself. You should count on the students to take about four times the amount of time it takes you to complete the test. You will have the best sense of how many items your students can tackle in a given period of time. There are some rules of thumb which, for basic MCQs, range from one to two minutes per MCQ for determining testing time. If you're using context-dependent item sets, or mixing formats, or using aids (like calculators), students may not be able to work as quickly. Again, we think you'll be the best judge. If you're really not sure, write a practice test of 30 items, and give it during a 10-minute class session. See how many items, on average, are completed.

If the student is allowed to use aids during the assessment (such as a calculator, notes, textbook), be sure to state *specifically* what is allowed. It should go without saying that this information should be communicated early and often to students, but it also needs to be formally included in the written instructions on the test.

Students should also be informed about the administration format for the assessment. Will the assessment be administered in the classroom or online? Are there any authentication requirements? For example, in a classroom setting, will students be required to show their college identification card before gaining access to the classroom? In the online setting, will students go to the university computer lab to take the assessment or will they be allowed to choose their location? If students can choose their location, will they be required to download and use specific software or hardware (e.g. webcam)? Refer to Figure 5.2 for a set of example instructions.

We're very purposefully avoiding a head-on treatment of the issues of cheating and test security. There are really good book-length treatments of those topics relevant to the college classroom (e.g. Cizek, 1999, 2003). And those topics, unfortunately, need their own books. Our point here is that,

---

Format: Online administration

Setting: Computer lab with a proctor

Question presentation: One at a time

Time allotment: 30 minutes

Instructions:

This multiple-choice quiz contains 10 questions, worth 2 points each for a total of 20 points. No deductions will be made for guessing. You will be given 30 minutes to complete the quiz so allot approximately 3 minutes per question. Some questions may take you more than 3 minutes and some less. You may **not** use a calculator, notes, or external websites during this assessment. Once the quiz begins your browser will be prevented from accessing any other website except for this assessment website.

You will be presented one question per page. Select the radio button next to each option (A, B, C, or D) to record your response. Click the "Next" button to move on to the next question or "Previous" to go back to the previous question. You may move back and forth between questions. When you have answered all of your questions click "Submit" on the last page to submit your quiz. If you do not click "Submit" before the 30-minute allotment expires, your responses completed up until that point will be automatically submitted for you.

To begin your assessment, click the "Begin" button below.

Figure 5.2 Example Instructions for an MCQ Online Assessment

whatever test-taking procedures you put in place, communicate early and often about them with your students. Doing so will enhance the meaning of the test scores (i.e. the validity) and will reduce test anxiety (a huge extraneous cognitive load).

Some students in your class may require accommodations during the assessment. Make sure that your approach is consistent with relevant laws (e.g. in the US, the Americans with Disabilities Act and the Individuals with Disabilities Education Act), and institutional and departmental policies. The processes by which students request an accommodation through formal or informal channels should be made clear well in advance of an assessment. This may be particularly true for online assessments which can require specialized software to be installed. Some accommodations require changes to the test administration procedures whereas others may require changes to the testing content itself. Consult with your local resources to determine how best to support students who require accommodations for your MCQ assessments.

Test Scoring

The ease of scoring MCQs is often seen as one of the primary advantages of this question type over tests that use short-answer or essay responses. While the most conventional approach to scoring a MCQ is to have one correct answer choice, there are other scoring strategies that can be used. We will explore approaches to differentially weighting questions or even answer choices within a question and when and why an instructor would want to use different scoring strategies. Additionally, we will review two approaches to using an overall assessment score to assign a grade.

Question Scoring Approaches

Typically, multiple-choice assessments are scored by using the Number Right method where correct answers are given some positive value, generally 1 point, and incorrect and unanswered questions are assigned a score of zero. A total score is calculated by summing the number of correct responses. This score can be converted to a percentage score by dividing the total score by the total number of questions on the assessment and multiplying by 100.

When in Doubt, Guess

One of the issues with the Number Right approach is that students can get a question correct by guessing. There have been several approaches to correct for guessing. One prominent approach is for students to lose points for incorrect answers, thereby discouraging guessing. Unanswered questions receive no points and incorrect answers receive a guessing "penalty" of $1/(n–1)$ when n equals the number of possible answer choices (Karandikar, 2010). This approach, often called Negative Marking, has been criticized for several reasons. First, it does not eliminate guessing and introduces error related to students' differences in risk-taking behaviors (Bar-Hillel *et al.*, 2005). Second, students who guess more frequently may benefit more so than students of equal ability who are reluctant to guess. Lastly, some instructors have recommended that students only guess when they can eliminate one or more distractors. It is challenging to determine how students will respond to instructions about guessing and it is unclear how to best advise students when the Negative Marking approach is used (Budescu and Bar-Hillel, 1993). This introduces a higher cognitive load, because now a student not only has to think about the content of the item but also has to weigh her probability of guessing and its consequences. It also might introduce a validity concern because some authors argue that using a Negative Marking approach to scoring multiple-choice assessments might measure students' answering strategies and risk-taking behavior instead of how well they know the content (Budescu and Bar-Hillel, 1993; Choppin, 1988).

Both Number Right and Negative Marking approaches do not take into account partial knowledge the student may have related to the learning objective being assessed by the MCQ (Bradbard *et al.*, 2004). Students often can eliminate options that they know are incorrect – even if you've got very plausible distractors. Student knowledge is seldom all or nothing. You may choose, therefore, to use a partial-credit scoring technique to give credit for what students do know.

Partial-Credit Scoring

Lesage, Valcke, and Sabbe (2013) outlined three main approaches to partial-credit scoring: the liberal multiple-choice approach which allows students to select more than one answer to a question; elimination testing, which instructs students to cross out all distractors they think are incorrect; and confidence weighting, where students select the option they think is correct and identify how confident they are about their selection. One scoring method in the liberal multiple-choice approach used with a five-choice MCQ awards 3 points for a single correct answer, 2 points for a correct answer with two choices selected and 1 point for a correct answer with three choices selected. Students are not given any points if four or more options are selected (Hobson and Ghoshal, 1996). The elimination testing method asks students to cross out, or eliminate, the options they think are incorrect. One point is awarded for each incorrect option that a student eliminates. However, a penalty is given if the correct answer is eliminated (for example, minus 3 in a four-option MCQ). Confidence weighting asks students to select what they think is the correct answer and how certain they are about their answer. One approach to scoring with confidence weighting is determined by multiplying the question weight (for example, 1) by the confidence level the student selected. For example, a MCQ worth 1 point and using a 3-point confidence scale (1 = a little confident, 2 = moderately confident, 3 = very confident) would receive anywhere from 1 to 3 points. An incorrect answer receives zero (confidence = 1), minus 2 (confidence = 2), or minus 6 (confidence = 3) points (Gardner-Medwin, 1995).

While partial-credit scoring methods might seem to positively address student partial knowledge and confidence issues, according to Bush (2001) no partial-credit scoring method has been found to outperform traditional multiple-choice scoring methods in terms of test reliability and validity evidence. This is yet another case of measurement goals and learning goals being in tension with each other.

Weighting Questions and Answer Choices

Another approach to addressing issues of partial knowledge is to differentially weight multiple-choice questions based on varying levels of importance. For example, if in a 10-question assessment five of your questions assess foundational learning objectives, you can assign those questions to be a higher weight. Those five questions could be worth 2 points each and the other five questions could be worth 1 point each, for a total of 15 possible points on the assessment. We mentioned this in the previous chapter on blueprints, also because these weights should ideally come from that level of thinking.

Item analysis information can also be used to determine weights. Questions that are more difficult can be assigned higher weights than those that are less difficult. One drawback of this approach is that this punishes students more severely for missing difficult questions. Wang and Stanley (1970) explored several approaches to weighting items and found that in general, weighting test questions shows little to no improvement in test reliability or validity, particularly for assessments with more than a few items. If you do differentially weight questions, you should clearly indicate for students how much weight each question is assigned. This communicates to students the relative importance of each question so they can adjust their effort accordingly. And, as we've argued elsewhere, you will also explain why some content is weighted more than other content. You can communicate this when you share the blueprint with students.

In addition to differentially weighting entire MCQs, another approach you can use is to differentially weight the correct answer and various distractors. In multiple-choice questions with weighted options, the key and distractors are weighted according to their approximate correctness. In addition to using your knowledge of the misconceptions and the level of "correctness" in each, known as judgement-based option weighting, you can use information from your item analysis to help you determine how or whether to weight answer choices, known as empirical option weighting (Frary, 1989). Distractors that are selected by a large number of students could be given higher weights than distractors that are selected by only a small number of students. Research has been mixed as to whether judgement-based and empirical option weighting approaches improve test reliability and validity (Frary, 1989). From a learning perspective, judgment-based option weighting is much more justifiable to students.

Another consideration is the weight you want to assign different question types. In Chapter 3 we discussed several variations on a MCQ, such as the matching item. A matching item that contains four premises is essentially four questions. You may want to give more weight to a matching question than a single multiple-choice MCQ. For example, the matching question with four premises might be worth 4 points and a MCQ on the same assessment might be worth 1 point. Or the MCQ might be worth 1 point and each premise on the matching question might be 0.25 point. With matching questions, you need to consider whether students will receive partial credit for each correct premise–response match, or will receive credit only if all of the matches are correct. In the former, it makes sense for you to weight each of the premises like a single item, or 4 points in our example. If students have to correctly match all of the premise–response pairs, you may want to consider weighting that question the same as a single MCQ. The binary choice item (true/false, yes/no, etc.) has only two options and therefore is the variation most susceptible to guessing. As a result, you may want to give less weight to questions of this type.

The option weighting approach is particularly appealing to Oliva Peña where some of her MCQs contain distractors that are somewhat correct but not the best choice. Olivia reviewed a question she previously administered where she felt weighted answer choices would be appropriate (see Figure 5.3).

Norm-Referenced vs. Criterion-Referenced Grading

Regardless of whether multiple-choice assessment questions are scored using the Number Right, Negative Marking, or other partial-credit approach, instructors often ask how to create a meaningful total score to assign grades.

The population in the United States in the Northeast region grew from over 4 million in 1820 to almost 11 million in 1860. However, the percentage of the population living in the Northeast dropped from 45% to 34% during that same time period. Which of the following best explains the drop in overall percentage of the population living in the northeastern United States from 1820 to 1860?

        a) Expansionism (4) **
        b) Immigration (2)
        c) Sectionalism (1)
        d) Urbanism (0)

Weighting rationale: During the 1820–1860 time period, a significant portion of the population moved to the Midwest and western United States and therefore expansionism (A) is the best answer. The overall population increase in both the Northeast and across all regions of the United States is attributable partly to immigration (B). However, the question focuses specifically on the drop in the overall percentage of the population living in the Northeast, not the growth in population numbers. Sectionalism (C) refers to different lifestyles, customs, and values of the various regions of the United States in the 1800s. While sectionalism could account for some shifting population trends, it is not the primary reason the Northeast saw a decline in overall percentage of the population. Urbanization is the population shift from rural to urban areas and is the opposite of what was happening in population changes during the 1800s as more individual moved westward toward more rural areas.

Figure 5.3 Example Weighted Answer Choices with Rationale

There are typically two methods for total assessment scoring: norm-referenced and criterion-referenced. Norm-referenced scoring is dependent on the performance of the particular group of students that completed the assessment. In this approach, grades are assigned based on a predetermined distribution. For example, the following normative scale could be used to assign grades:

Top 15 percent = A
Next 15 percent = B
Next 45 percent = C
Next 15 percent = D
Bottom 10 percent = F

Norm-referenced grading is often used when differentiation among students is critically important, such as in a "gatekeeper" course where only the top performers in the class can progress on to the subsequent course. This scoring approach is generally appropriate in large classes but more challenging to apply in small classes under about 50 students. Often known as "curving", norm-referenced grading can standardize grades so that the distribution of grades is comparable from year to year for an instructor or across instructors who teach the same course but use different MCQs on their assessments. The major disadvantage of this approach is that students' grades are determined not only by their knowledge of the content but also how well they compare to the performance of their peers, often creating a culture of competition among students in the class.

In contrast, criterion-referenced grading is based on predefined thresholds set by the instructor and there is no set number or percentage of students that are limited to reaching this threshold. For example, the following criteria could be used to assign grades:

92 percent – 100 percent = A
82 percent – 91 percent = B
72 percent – 81 percent = C
62 percent – 71 percent = D
Below 62 percent = F

Criterion-referenced grading measures how well students have met the various learning objectives in the assessment, and since all students can theoretically attain the top threshold this eliminates competition among students. One disadvantage of criterion-referenced grading is that instructors may have to adjust the criteria to account for a particularly difficult assessment. For example, if no students reached the "A" threshold on an assessment it could be that the questions used were too difficult or had problems. This requires adjusting students' grades to account for issues with the assessment.

Regardless of whether you use a norm-referenced or criterion-referenced grading approach, you should make your grading policy clear to students at the very start of your class. Dawn has consulted with countless instructors whose primary complaint is students who argue about grades. Using the principles from this book to create high-quality MCQs will help combat some (but unfortunately not all!) of the issues often raised by students.

Summary

Using these strategies for constructing, administering and scoring your MCQ assessment will help make the process smoother for you and your students, since expectations will be clear for everyone from the beginning!

References and Resources for Further Reading

American Educational Research Association, American Psychological Association, and National Council on Measurement in Education (2014). *Standards for Educational and Psychological Testing*. Washington, DC: American Educational Research Association.

Bar-Hillel, M., Budescu, D., and Attali, Y. (2005). Scoring and keying multiple choice tests: A case study in irrationality. *Mind & Society*, 4, 3–12.

Bradbard, D. A., Parker, D. F., and Stone, G. L. (2004). An alternate multiple-choice scoring procedure in a macroeconomics course. *Decision Sciences Journal of Innovative Education*, 2(1), 11–26.

Budescu, D. and Bar-Hillel, M. (1993). To guess or not to guess: A decision-theoretic view of formula scoring. *Journal of Educational Measurement*, 30(4), 277–91.

Bush, M. (2001). A multiple choice test that rewards partial knowledge. *Journal of Further and Higher Education*, 25(2), 157–63.

Carlson, J. L. and Ostrosky, A. L. (1992). Item sequence and student performance on multiple-choice exams: Further evidence. *Journal of Economic Education*, 23, 232–5. doi:10.2307/1183225

Choppin, B. H. (1988). Correction for guessing. In J. P. Keeves (ed.) *Educational Research, Methodology, and Measurement: An international handbook* (384–6). Oxford: Pergamon Press.

Cizek, G. (1999). *Cheating on Tests: How to do it, detect it, and prevent it*. New York, NY: Routledge.

Cizek, G. (2003). *Detecting and Preventing Classroom Cheating: Promoting integrity in assessment*. Thousand Oaks, CA: Corwin Press.

Covington, M. V. and Omelich, C. L. (1987). 'I knew it cold before the exam': A test of the anxiety blockage hypothesis. *Journal of Educational Psychology*, 79, 393–400.

Frary, R. B. (1989). Partial-credit scoring methods for multiple-choice tests. *Applied Measurement in Education*, 2(1), 79–96.

Gardner-Medwin, A. R. (1995). Confidence assessment in the teaching of basic science. *Association for Learning Technology Journal*, 3, 80–5.

Gohmann, S. F. and Spector, L. C. (1989). Test scrambling and student performance. *Journal of Economic Education*, 20, 235–8. doi:10.2307/1182298

Gronlund, N. E. (1988). *How to Construct Achievement Tests* (4th ed.). Englewood Cliffs, NJ: Prentice Hall.

Hobson, A. and Ghoshal, D. (1996). Flexible scoring for multiple-choice exams. *The Physics Teacher*, 34, 284.

Huntley, R. M. and Welch, C. J. (1993). Numerical answer options: Logical or random order? Paper presented at the American Educational Research Association, Atlanta, GA.

Leary, L. F. and Dorans, N. J. (1985). Implications for altering the context in which test items appear: A historical perspective on an immediate concern. *Review of Educational Research*, 55, 387–413.

Lesage, E., Valcke, M., and Sabbe, E. (2013). Scoring methods for multiple choice assessment in higher education – Is it still a matter of number right scoring or negative marking? *Studies in Educational Evaluation*, 39(3), 188–93. http://dx.doi.org/10.1016/j.stueduc.2013.07.001

Karandikar, R. L. (2010). On multiple choice tests and negative marking. *Current Science*, 99(8), 1042–5.

Miller, C. (2011). Aesthetics and e-assessment: The interplay of emotional design and learner performance. *Distance Education*, 32(3), 307–37.

Newman, D. L., Kundert, D. K., Lane, D. S., and Sather Bull, K. (1988). Effect of varying item order on multiple-choice test scores: Importance of statistical and cognitive difficulty. *Applied Measurement in Education*, 1(1), 89–97.

Sweller, J. (1994). Cognitive load theory, learning difficulty and instructional design. *Learning and Instruction*, 4, 295–312.

Wang, M. W. and Stanley, J. C. (1970). Differential weighting: A review of methods and empirical studies. *Review of Educational Research*, 40(5), 663–705. www.jstor.org/stable/1169462

6   Improving Your Tests

One of the main advantages of using multiple-choice questions is that you can obtain statistical information about how well an individual question or set of questions is working. Typically, this statistical information is referred to as an item analysis. Understanding how to interpret and use information based on an item analysis is as important as knowing how to construct a well-designed MCQ. You can use this information not only to inform you about how well your students are learning, but also to guide and inform your instruction. Item analysis can come in useful for the current exam, for follow-up to the current exam, or for the next time you use these particular items.

We're going to show you some of the commonly used formulas for doing item analysis. Note two things. First, there are other formulas and approaches to each of these analyses, so you may see others elsewhere. Second, if you're machine-scoring your tests in any way, the software you're using is likely to produce these statistics for you. So you probably won't actually have to compute these for yourself.

How Difficult Are Your Questions?

The first statistic included in an item analysis is the *item difficulty*. This measurement term has a very specific, narrow definition and shouldn't be overgeneralized. In measurement terminology, item difficulty, often referred to as the p-value, is the percentage of students that correctly answered the question. That is a very useful number to have but may not actually mean that students found the item hard or challenging (we'll explain further in a moment). The p-value is calculated by dividing the number of students who got the question correct by the total number of students who answered the question. It ranges from 0 percent to 100 percent, but more typically is written as a proportion from 0.0 to 1.0. The higher the p-value, the *easier* the item. For example, a p-value of 0.30 indicates that 30 percent of the students who answered that question got it correct (a relatively difficult item) whereas a p-value of 0.75 indicates that 75 percent of the students answered it correctly (a relatively easy item).

How difficult should your MCQs be for students? That is, what is an ideal item difficulty? We really have to juxtapose measurement considerations here against learning and learner considerations to reach an answer, or more importantly, to use item difficulty values to make decisions about an item. Let's back up to one of the reasons we're giving this test, and thus these items, in the first place. We're using a test to find out what students know and what they don't know of the required course content. Put a different way, we're trying to differentiate those students who do know the content represented in a particular MCQ from those students who do not know that content. For that purpose, and for technical measurement reasons we won't bore you with here, the "ideal" item difficulty is 0.50. That is, a MCQ that half of the students get right and half of the students get wrong provides maximum differentiation among students. But if your test were constructed only of such items, the average test score would be 50 percent. You don't have to use your imagination very long to know how your classes would react to that (and perhaps your colleagues and department chair!). You are also actively teaching, and you wouldn't feel very efficacious as a teacher if the average score came in at 50 percent. If we've taught well and our students learned well, shouldn't the average p-value across all items for the test be more like 90 percent? We're thus in a conundrum of competing goals. The compromise usually taken here, then, is that the ideal p-value is slightly higher than midway between chance (1.00 divided by the number of options) and a perfect score (1.00) for the question. For a four-option multiple-choice question the ideal value is 0.74 (74 percent) and for a five-option multiple-choice question the ideal value is 0.70 (70 percent) (Lord, 1952).

There are some general guidelines when interpreting item difficulty values for your MCQs. P-values above 0.90 are very easy items and generally should not be reused again for subsequent assessments because they are not good differentiators. If almost all of the students can get the item correct, it is a concept probably not worth testing. One caveat to this guideline is when you want to ensure that all or almost all of the students correctly understand a concept. You might have a core learning objective that is a foundation for your course and you want a high percentage of students correctly answering the question. You may also have reporting purposes, such as for outcomes assessment or accreditation purposes, for which you need to show mastery of a student learning objective.

At the low end of the range, p-values below 0.30 are very difficult questions and the key issue is, "What made it hard for students to get it right?" It could be something about the question itself, these students' particular course experience, or about their learning. Such items should be reviewed for possible confusing language, removed from subsequent assessments, and/or highlighted as an area for re-instruction. If almost all of the students get the question wrong there is either a problem with the question or students did not get the concept. The first step is to review the question stem: was it written clearly? Did it address a single concept? The second step is to explore the distractors: were they written succinctly to address a common student misconception? Was there an answer choice that could have been confusing or misleading? Are there two correct answers? If there seem to be construction issues, you could actually modify student scores based on this analysis. A popular option is to give everyone who took the test one question's worth of points; that is, to "throw out" the item. We advocate a more nuanced approach, however. If the p-value was 0.20, 20 percent of the students have already received credit for this question, so giving everybody credit double-credits these students. We advocate giving everyone who got the item wrong credit for this item. This can take a little explaining, but students typically grasp how this approach is fair.

If you explore the question construction and there seem to be no issues, this could be a challenging concept that the students in your class did not understand. This is an opportunity for you to provide additional instruction before moving on. You included the question in an assessment to address an important learning objective, so ensuring that most of the students understand the concept is a critical component of your instruction!

We believe that fairness and the meaning of the test scores dictate that you have an obligation to adjust scores if you determine that you have a flawed question. Once you've addressed the issue for this test, though, you also need to alter the item for its next use so the same problem doesn't arise.

Another consideration when examining item difficulty statistics is the pattern across the entire test. Too many hard items tend to demoralize less able students and too many easy items tend to bore more able students. So from a motivation standpoint, a blend of easy and hard is desirable. For all the reasons we've discussed so far, it may make the most sense to have an average item difficulty of all the items on the test in that 0.70 ballpark. That tends to be the point that best blends the measurement and learning considerations.

How Well Do Your Questions Discriminate?

The second statistic typically included in an item analysis is the *item discrimination*, which is the point-biserial relationship between how well students did on the question and their total score on the assessment. Discrimination, in this context, does not have the negative connotation it has in more general usage; in fact, discrimination here is a very good thing and lies at the heart of good assessment. We just explained above that good measurement means being able to differentiate those who know from those who don't. Item discrimination indices are numerical representations of how well that differentiation is working. Figure 6.1 shows how the item discrimination value is calculated.

As with any correlation value, the range is from −1.00 to 1.00. The higher the value, the more discriminating the question. A highly discriminating question indicates that the students who had high assessment scores got the question correct whereas students who had low test scores got the question

$$\frac{(\overline{X}_C - \overline{X}_T)}{SD\ Total} \sqrt{\frac{p}{q}} \quad \text{where}$$

$\overline{X}_C$ = the mean total score for persons who have responded correctly to the question

$\overline{X}_T$ = the mean total score for all persons

p = the difficulty value for the question

$q = (1 - p)$

SD Total = the standard deviation of total assessment scores

Figure 6.1 Item Discrimination Formula

incorrect. Theoretically, the closer the item discrimination value is to 1.00 the better. When we take the learner and learning into account, as well as some of the practicalities of how items tend to work, a more acceptable range is generally 0.20 or higher.

When reviewing your item analysis results, questions with discrimination values *near to or less than zero* should be removed from the assessment because they are not measuring well and likely have flaws. This indicates that students who overall did poorly on the assessment did *better* on that question than students who overall did well. The question may be confusing for your better scoring students in some way.

Is Your Test Reliable?

A third component of the item analysis is the *reliability coefficient*. The reliability coefficient is a measure of the amount of measurement error associated with an assessment score. Note that a single reliability coefficient is calculated not for each item but for the total score on the assessment. Reliability is the property of a test score, not usually of an individual item. Typically, the internal consistency reliability is measured. This indicates how well the items are correlated with one another. With multiple-choice questions that are scored correct/incorrect, the Kuder-Richardson formula 20 (KR-20) is often used to calculate the internal consistency reliability.

The reliability coefficient range is from 0.00 to 1.00. The higher the value, the more reliable the overall assessment score. For classroom assessments, the acceptable range is generally around 0.60 or higher. For higher stakes assessments, such as standardized exams used for college admissions, reliability coefficients tend to be 0.90 or higher. High reliability values indicate that the scores are trustworthy, that they consistently represent mastery (or not!) of the content. Lots of different aspects of the test can influence the reliability, and, even more problematically, can interact with one another to influence the reliability. For example, tests with lots of items tend to have better reliability than tests with fewer items. The higher the average item discrimination indices are, the higher the reliability will be. And those two things can feed into each other. Note again, that measurement considerations and learning considerations can play against one another with an "acceptable" reliability.

$$\frac{K}{K-1}(1-\frac{\sum pq}{\sigma^2_x}) \quad \text{where}$$

K = number of questions
p = proportion of persons who responded correctly to a question (i.e. difficulty value)
q = proportion of persons who responded incorrectly to a question (i.e. $1 - p$)
σ^2_x = total score variance

Figure 6.2 KR-20 Formula for Internal Consistency Reliability

How Well Did Your Distractors Work?

Once you are ready, either live (that is, in a way which will affect scores on this particular test occasion) or for the future, to explore why items worked well or worked poorly, the most useful statistical tool is distractor evaluation. As defined earlier, the distractors are the incorrect alternatives in a multiple-choice question. The quality of the distractors influences student performance on an assessment item. Although the correct answer must be truly correct, it is just as important that the distractors be incorrect. Distractors should appeal to low scorers who have not mastered the material, whereas high scorers should infrequently select the distractors. Reviewing the options can reveal potential errors of judgment and inadequate performance of distractors. These poor distractors can be revised, replaced, or removed in ways that either affect current scores or future use of the item.

One way to study responses to distractors is with a frequency table. This table tells you the number and/or percentage of students that selected each distractor. Distractors that are selected by a few or no students should be removed or replaced. Such distractors are just serving as passive camouflage, at best, and may simply be a waste of ink. As a general guideline, look for distractors selected by five or fewer students, assuming you have at least 50 students in your class. These kinds of distractors are likely to be so implausible to students that hardly anyone selects them. One distractor that is selected by as many or more students than the correct answer may indicate a confusing question and/or options. Occasionally, studying the distractor analysis may reveal that you simply wrote the key down wrongly on your scoring key.

While many item analysis programs report frequency table information aggregated across all students, some also provide a breakdown of responses (and item difficulty) by students' overall test score. Depending on the number of students who completed the assessment, the total score distribution is split into two to five subgroups, each with an approximately equal number of students. In Table 6.1, you can see a frequency distribution divided into four equal subgroups.

You can see that the top subgroup (#1) more often selected the correct answer (D) than did the last subgroup (#4). Ideally, you should see a decrease in the number of students who answer the question correctly as you move

Table 6.1 Distractor Frequency Distribution Split by Student Overall Score

	A	B	C	D	E	p-value	TOTAL N
1 (75–99 percentile)	0	9	1	183	0	0.88	208
2 (50–74 percentile)	9	47	6	148	0	0.71	208
3 (25–49 percentile)	11	55	12	126	4	0.61	208
4 (1–24 percentile)	10	76	20	109	7	0.53	207
TOTAL	30	187	37	566	11	0.68	831

from the first to the last subgroup. This pattern should be reversed for the distractors in that the top students in subgroup 1 should be less likely to select the incorrect options compared to students in the subsequent subgroups.

Earlier, we encouraged you to write distractors using student misconceptions. This is where that really pays off because one possibility, if few students are selecting one distractor, is that few students share that misconception. This is yet another example of where the measurement principle and the learning principle can be at odds. A distractor chosen by few students isn't helping you with your measurement purpose of differentiating students but it is informative from a learning perspective.

Technical Qualities of MCQ Variations

As we mentioned in Chapter 3 on variations, there are several alternatives to the traditional three to five options for multiple-choice questions, including matching, binary choice, context-dependent item sets, vignettes, and the complex multiple-choice (Type K) question types. The technical qualities in terms of difficulty, discrimination, and overall contribution to test reliability tends to work well for most of these variations *except* for the Type K question type, which has a set of responses and the answer choices contain various combinations of those responses (A and B, A and C, B and D, etc.). Research suggests that the Type K format is more difficult than conventional multiple-choice format (Haladyna and Downing, 1989). Additionally, because all possible combinations of responses are not always used in the answer choices, students are often cued into the correct answer; for example, when three of the four choices contain response "A". This cueing tends to negatively affect the reliability of the item (Albanese, 1993). Exploring the technical qualities of the MCQ and its variations can help you build a stronger assessment.

Sample Item Analysis

Dr. Shah learned that the assessment software she was using to administer her online quizzes provided item analysis information. In Figure 6.3 is the item analysis report she received on her first quiz which contained ten multiple-choice questions.

Item Analysis (10 questions) – correct answer (key) is in **bold**								

Number of students = 831

Mean score = 60.4

Reliability = 0.64

ITEM	p-value	Discrimination value	A	B	C	D	E
1.	0.68	0.35	30	187	37	**566**	11
2.	0.89	0.20	**739**	5	1	9	77
3.	0.55	0.37	4	233	46	88	**460**
4.	0.99	-0.05	**822**	3	3	3	0
5.	0.93	0.13	24	0	12	**775**	20
6.	0.74	-0.02	25	16	**615**	35	140
7.	0.40	0.33	68	107	**334**	165	157
8.	0.26	0.09	114	168	**213**	160	176
9.	0.14	0.03	75	64	**120**	67	505
10.	0.46	0.45	**379**	98	74	83	197

Figure 6.3 Sample Item Analysis

Dr. Shah wanted some help interpreting the item analysis so she met with a consultant at her institution's assessment center. The first area the consultant and Dr. Shah examined was the item difficulty. They looked for very easy (above 0.90) or very hard (below 0.30) questions. Based on those guidelines they flagged questions 4 and 5 (too easy) and 8 and 9 (too hard). Next they reviewed the item discrimination values to see which questions did not meet the recommended minimum value of 0.20. Questions 4, 5, 8, and 9 also stood out, as did question 6. Lastly, they looked at the frequency distribution to see which distractors had fewer than five students select them. The questions that had problematic distractors were: question 2, distractor C; question 3, distractor A; question 4, distractors A, C, D, and E; and question 5, distractor B. Pulling all of the item analysis information together, Dr. Shah and the consultant decided to thoroughly review the following questions:

- Question 2, distractor C
- Question 3, distractor A
- Question 4, distractors A, C, D, and E; high p-value; low discrimination

---

Question 2: A group of 100 students is given an IQ test and the distribution has a mean of 100 and a standard deviation of 15. If every student's IQ score is divided by 5, what would be the standard deviation of the distribution?

   a) 3**
   b) 5
   c) 9 *(number of students selecting this option = 1)*
   d) 10
   e) 15

Figure 6.4 Question 2 from Sample Item Analysis

- Question 5, distractor B; high p-value, low discrimination
- Question 6, low discrimination
- Question 8, low p-value
- Question 9, low p-value

The good news is that it looks like questions 1, 7, and 10 worked well! Since this was Dr. Shah's first online MCQ assessment, the consultant informed her that it's not surprising that several of the questions need some review.

In Dr. Shah's review of question 2 (Figure 6.4), she sees that it is unlikely for students to select option C (9) as it does not address a common misconception or error. The question worked reasonably well and most of the students got the question correct, so there is no need to make any adjustments for the scoring on this current assessment. However, Dr. Shah agrees that she needs to remove or revise this distractor if she uses this question again in the future.

After reviewing the problematic distractor for question 3 (Figure 6.5), Dr. Shah sees that there was a typo in this distractor. It should have read "The z-score distribution will have a mean of 50 and a standard deviation of 10." She will update the question for the next time she uses it.

The consultant working with Dr. Shah informs her that when a question has a very high p-value, as is the case with question 4 (Figure 6.6), by default the discrimination value will be low and very few distractors will be selected

---

Question 3: A negatively skewed distribution of scores with a mean of 50 and a standard deviation of 10 has been transformed into z-scores. Which of the following is correct about the distribution of z-scores?

   a) The z-score distribution will have a mean of 5 and a standard deviation of 10 *(number selecting this option = 4)*
   b) The z-score distribution will have a mean of 0 and a standard deviation of -1
   c) The z-score distribution will have the same mean and standard deviation as the original distribution
   d) The distribution of z-scores will have a normally-shaped distribution
   e) The z-score distribution will have a mean of 0 and a standard deviation of 1**

Figure 6.5 Question 3 from Sample Item Analysis

Question 4: Which of the following z-scores is <u>furthest</u> from the mean of a distribution?
a) −2.60**
b) +1.50
c) 0.00
d) −1.80
e) +2.40

Figure 6.6 Question 4 from Sample Item Analysis

since almost all of the students got the question correct. Dr. Shah reviewed the question and decided that the question addresses a core learning objective in her course and that having almost all the students get the question correct is critical to their progressing through the course.

After looking at question 5 (Figure 6.7), Dr. Shah decides that the question as written is too easy and the distractors, particularly option B, do not address common student misconceptions. She decides that she will revise the distractors for this question for future iterations.

Question 5: A student receives a 690 on the quantitative section of her GRE exam which places her in the 89th percentile. Which of the following is the best interpretation of her percentile rank?

a) The student scored equal to or better than 11% of other students who took the GRE quantitative section.

b) The student scored equal to or better than 94.5% of other students who took the GRE quantitative section.

c) The student scored equal to or better than 5.5% of other students who took the GRE quantitative section.

d) The student scored equal to or better than 89% of other students who took the GRE quantitative section.**

e) The student scored 89% correct on the GRE quantitative section.

Figure 6.7 Question 5 from Sample Item Analysis

Question 6: Which of the following is an advantage of transforming raw scores into z-scores?

a) Skewed distributions can be transformed into a normal distribution using z-scores

b) z-score transformation reduces a distribution's variability

c) You can compare scores from two distributions that have been transformed to z-scores**

d) z-scores normalize the frequency distribution

e) You can determine the relative position of groups of scores from the mean

Figure 6.8 Question 6 from Sample Item Analysis

Question 8: Why would you want to convert z-scores into a standardized distribution with a given mean and standard deviation?

    a) The standard deviation and the variance of a z-score are equals
    b) z-scores cannot be compared unless they are converted to a standardized distribution
    c) A standardized distribution can remove negative values often found with z-scores**
    d) If the z-score is calculated from a weighted mean it will skew the distribution unless it is converted
    e) Since the standard deviation is one, the z-scores must be converted in order to calculate the variance

Figure 6.9 Question 8 from Sample Item Analysis

The discrimination value for question 6 (Figure 6.8) indicates that the students who did better overall on the quiz performed worse on this question than the students who did not perform well on the quiz. It appears that these students may have selected option E. Dr. Shah agrees that option E could be a correct answer as well, and both option C and option E should be scored as correct. She works with the consultant to revise the scores in the online assessment system to give credit to those students who selected option E for this question.

In looking at the distribution of answer choices for question 8 (Figure 6.9), it appears that about an equal number of students selected each distractor and the correct answer. The consultant advises Dr. Shah that this pattern is often indicative of students guessing. Dr. Shah considers the question and reflects that students struggled with the concept of a standardized distribution as reflected in their activities and homework assignments. The question high-lights an area on which Dr. Shah will need to provide additional instruction. She plans to post some additional explanations, examples, and practice ques-tions for her online course to ensure her students have grasped this concept.

Dr. Shah realizes that most students selected option E in question 9 (Figure 6.10) because in a *normal* distribution, which is symmetric, the mean,

Question 9: In a symmetric distribution, which of the following is the best measure of central tendency?

    a) Mean
    b) Median
    c) Mode**
    d) Median or mode
    e) Mean, median, or mode

Figure 6.10 Question 9 from Sample Item Analysis

median, or mode are all the same, and therefore would be the best choice. However, a symmetric distribution is not always necessarily normal in shape (e.g. a symmetric, bimodal distribution). Dr. Shah realizes that this subtle distinction may not have been clear to students and therefore this question became a trick question of sorts. She decides to award credit for option E and to revise the question stem to be clearer for future uses.

Summary

In addition to determining whether to rescore or provide additional instruction related to questions on a given assessment, item analysis information can also be used for future administrations using the same MCQs. Provided a sufficient number of students answered the question (at least 50), the MCQ should have similar difficulty and discrimination values when administered to a different group of students in another semester. Additionally, the average score on an assessment should approximately equal the average difficulty across all MCQs when administered to a sufficiently large sample of students. Therefore, if you reuse MCQs in quizzes or exams across semesters you can construct an assessment where you have a reasonable estimate of the average score on the assessment *before* you administer it.

References and Resources for Further Reading

Albanese, M. A. (1993). Type K and other complex multiple-choice items: An analysis of research and item properties. *Educational Measurement: Issues and Practice*, 12(1), 28–33.

DeVellis, R. F. (1991). *Scale Development: Theory and applications*. Newbury Park: Sage Publications.

Haladyna, T. M. (1999). *Developing and Validating Multiple-Choice Test Items* (2nd ed.). Mahwah, NJ: Lawrence Erlbaum Associates.

Haladyna, T. M. and Downing, S. M. (1989). Validity of a taxonomy of multiple-choice item-writing rules. *Applied Measurement in Education*, 2(1), 51–78.

Lord, F. M. (1952). The relationship of the reliability of multiple-choice test to the distribution of item difficulties. *Psychometrika*, 18, 181–94.

Suen, H. K. (1990). *Principles of Test Theories*. Hillsdale, NJ: Lawrence Erlbaum Associates.

Section III

MCQs and Leveraging Technology

7 Online Assessment Using MCQs

While the multiple-choice question is not new, advances in educational technologies have significantly improved what can be included in a multiple-choice question and how and when an assessment is delivered. This is a big reason why we argued in Chapter 1 that MCQs are actually wonderfully flexible and can be rich learning experiences for your students, not simply dry, antiseptic measurement probes. Delivering MCQs online has advantages and drawbacks that range from offering adaptive learning approaches to concerns about authentication and cheating. The technology also opens up fabulous learning opportunities to deliver targeted, immediate feedback to students at relatively much less time, energy, and money. We will discuss the pros and cons of when and how to deliver MCQs through online assessment technologies in this chapter and the possibilities for feedback in a subsequent chapter.

Variations from Paper-and-Pencil MCQs

Traditional paper-based assessments previously limited you to creating multiple-choice questions with text and static images, but the ubiquitous availability of assessment software programs and mobile devices such as laptops, tablets, and smartphones on which to deliver assessments now allows you to include media in multiple-choice questions. The ability to include media such as graphics, audio, and video into the question stem and response choices expands the knowledge and skills you can assess with a MCQ.

Graphics can range from static images to more sophisticated animations and simulations. Students can interact with a simulation as a part of the question stem and the distractors might contain text, numbers, or images from which the students can select. Sam Oliver is particularly interested in taking advantage of the affordances technology has to offer him to enhance his multiple-choice questions. He created a simulation on human population growth since the 1600s and wants his students to be able to identify the factors that are affecting population growth and to predict future growth.

Question: Which of the following is a phrase that might be used to ask a stranger how he is doing?

Answer choices (audio clips would be provided in lieu of the text answers below)

a) Comment allez-vous?**

b) Ça va?

c) Tu vas bien?

d) Quoi de neuf?

Figure 7.1 Example MCQ That Could Use Audio Clips

Sam thinks he can write some multiple-choice questions to correspond to the simulation to ensure that they are getting the foundational concepts and then can use students' answers to inform his classroom discussion on the topic.

In addition to graphics, you can embed audio clips in the question stem and/or responses in most online quizzing software or learning management systems. Suppose you teach a second-language course and you want to assess your students' ability to comprehend pronunciation, conversation, or appropriate phrasing in that language. In the question stem, you could ask students to listen to a clip of someone posing a question in the topic language and provide corresponding text or audio clips that would answer the question (Figure 7.1).

Video clips can also be used to assess content that can be difficult to represent in text. Dawn has worked with instructors who use video to present scenarios with answer choices in American Sign Language courses for which multiple-choice questions previously were not an option. Video has also been used to present mock clips of situations such as counseling sessions, patient–practitioner interactions, and courtroom arguments. Such possibilities overcome some of the major criticisms of MCQs about whether they can get to higher-order thinking and whether they can tap performance-oriented learning outcomes.

Addressing Cheating Concerns

While there are several advantages of using online technologies for your MCQs, you might be asking, "What about the potential for cheating online?" You share some of the same concerns as Dr. Peña. Her department chair has already raised concerns about cheating in the introductory history class and the last thing Olivia wants to do is increase this behavior by using online assessments. There are technology solutions to help with that, as well. If you are delivering your online assessment outside of the classroom, there are new authentication methods being developed. These include keystroke recognition, webcam proctoring, and biometric techniques like palm vein recognition (Sandeen, 2013). These technology solutions all come at a cost, so you should weigh the need for authentication with your purpose for giving the assessment.

Assuming you can authenticate the student providing answers to your multiple-choice assessment, how do you know they are not sitting next to a friend also in your class and answering the questions together? Webcam proctoring would give you the ability to view the student's physical location, but that type of proctoring may be best suited for high-stakes situations where individual performance is essential. In other situations, you may just want to ensure that the student is doing her own work. Some colleges and universities employ an Honor Code approach which requires students to sign or otherwise certify that they did their own work and did not cheat in any way.

There are several helpful features in how MCQs can be administered online that address cheating concerns. Many assessment systems allow you to present questions one page at a time or all on the same page. Additionally, you can scramble the order of the questions so that even if all students receive the same set of questions they will not receive them in the same order. You can also randomize the order that the distractors are presented so students seeing the same question would have the answer choices in a different order. You may be able to specify that once students have answered a question they cannot return to it, which may be particularly helpful for MCQs whose order you have elected to scramble. Some assessment systems allow you to set time limits for completing each question or for the assessment as a whole. If you do elect to set time limits, make sure to provide enough time for students to adequately answer all the questions, so that you are primarily testing your learning objectives and not how quickly students can answer MCQs. As a rule of thumb, students should be given one to two minutes per question, with more time allotted if the question requires a significant amount of reading or calculations. Such options have always been available to instructors, but the technology has made it much less labor intensive, now nearly trivial, to deploy these tactics.

Olivia knows that she wants to give online quizzes at the end of each lesson and has elected to present one question per page, scramble the question and answer choice order, and provide a time limit for the entire quiz. She does not want to prohibit students from going back and forth between questions, since she knows students often like to skip around and reflect on their work before completing a quiz. After all, reviewing one's work is a foundational learning strategy that we should encourage our students to employ. Oliva is struggling with whether or not to give all the students the same set of questions or to create different versions of her quiz. Learn more about which strategy Olivia should use in Chapter 8!

Summary

You'll need to weigh the pros and cons of online assessment in deciding if this is for you. There are some tremendous advantages to using technology, but also some significant drawbacks as well that need to be balanced. The next few chapters explore ways in which technology is evolving to support your development of MCQs into a more effective learning and assessment tool.

References and Resources for Further Reading

Sandeen, C. (2013). Assessment's place in the new MOOC world. *Research & Practice in Assessment*, 8(2), 5–12.

8   Scaling Up

Dr. Shah is concerned about using the same MCQs in her online quizzes and exams for a class of several hundred students. She worries that students will cheat, as even the most honorable students might be tempted to do so in a completely online class. However, she knows that the online assessment software system at her institution includes an "item bank" feature, where each student receives a different question on the same concept. We will explore when and how instructors would want to use item banks with MCQs in their assessments.

Writing Parallel Questions

One advantage of multiple-choice questions is that often an instructor can create parallel questions. Two parallel multiple-choice questions essentially have the same characteristics – they are equally difficult for students and differentiate between students with high knowledge and low knowledge on that concept in the same way. It is also possible to use templates that make item-writing more efficient. For example, look at the two different algebraic equations in Figure 8.1.

In both cases, the problem requires the same process to answer the question, and has the same correct answer (2), but each student receives what appears to be a different problem. You can create "pools" of items that measure the same skill at the same level of difficulty and set the delivery software to randomly select questions from each pool. The order of the questions and answer choices can also be randomized. In this way, each student receives a unique assessment that can minimize the effects of cheating. Creating parallel MCQs can be a daunting task, particularly for more conceptual questions, but hopefully these resources will help, should you find you want to do this!

As the two examples in Figure 8.1 demonstrate, creating parallel multiple-choice questions for content like math or statistics can be fairly straightforward. A common procedure or principle can be used with variable numerical values. Some software programs will often allow numerical values in an equation or problem to be randomized. For example, a range of values can be set as in Figure 8.2.

Student A: What is the appropriate value of 'x' when solving the following equation?

2x + 3 = 7

   a) –2
   b) 2**
   c) 5
   d) 8

Student B: What is the appropriate value of 'x' when solving the following equation?

3x + 1 = 7

   a) –2
   b) 2**
   c) 2 2/3
   d) 18

Figure 8.1 Example Parallel Math MCQs

[2 to 4]x + [3 to 5] = [7 to 10]

Figure 8.2 Example Question with Randomized Values

However, instructors like Olivia Peña worry about how to create item banks that have effective parallel items to ensure fair and representative questions for all her students. The most critical component of writing parallel MCQs is to ensure that the same learning objective or skill is being assessed in the question as outlined in your test blueprint. As the section below on item shells demonstrates, you can use a different stem (scenario) with the same distractors or use the same stem and key with different distractors. You are more likely to obtain similar questions when you can vary the scenario of the questions and keep the same or similar stem and distractors. Olivia took a stab at trying this and developed the two questions shown in Figure 8.3.

Item Shells

Another strategy for forming parallel items is creating item shells (Haladyna and Shindoll, 1989; Haladyna 2004). An item shell is "a 'hollow' item containing a syntactic structure that is useful for writing sets of similar items" (Haladyna and Shindoll, 1989). "What is the definition of … ?", "What is the most or least important … ?", and "Which is an example of … ?" are all very basic shells. Haladyna (2004) demonstrated the ingenious and elegant approach of adapting a successful item into an item template that can then be used to create additional items. In Figure 8.4 we use Haladyna's steps but illustrate with our own example, an item we used in Chapter 3.

Learning objective: Students will be able to identify the impact that the Great Famine of Ireland in the 1840s had on the massive influx of Irish immigrants coming to the United States.

Question 1A: How did the Great Famine of Ireland in the 1840s primarily impact the United States?

    a) A massive wave of Irish immigrants fled to the United States. **
    b) The influence of the Roman Catholic Church in the United States decreased.
    c) The United States increased financial support to Ireland.
    d) Potato imports from all countries declined.

Question 1B: A massive wave of Irish immigrants came to the United States in the 1840s as a result of which of the following?

    a) The Great Famine of Ireland **
    b) Persecution from the Roman Catholic Church in Ireland
    c) Increased financial support from the United States for Irish immigrants
    d) The increasingly strained relationship between Ireland and the British Crown.

Figure 8.3 Example Parallel History MCQs

Which individual with an interest in events in Boston in 1773 would most likely have thought that the Boston Team Party was an ill-advised provocation of the British Parliament?

    a) Joyce Junior, an anonymous patriot handbill writer
    b) Massachusetts' Royal Governor Thomas Hutchinson
    c) Benjamin Franklin, agent for the Massachusetts in London**
    d) British General Thomas Gage

Figure 8.4 Example of Deriving an Item Shell from an Existing Item

Haladyna's first step is to choose a stem from a successful item. Successful, here, means one that matches your learning outcomes well, and has acceptable item difficulty and item discrimination on a previous administration.

The second step is to identify the key words or issues in the stem; we've underlined several. The goal in this step is to identify the components of the basic, underlying structure of the item. The underlying structure here is: Someone ("individual") in some place ("Boston") at some time ("1773") holds a view ("ill-advised provocation") of a particular event ("Boston Tea Party"). Who is that someone?

Step three is to develop variations on these keywords. For this same historical period, "someone" could be other individuals, or it could also be groups of people: the British Parliament; the Sons of Liberty; the Massachusetts Royal Governor; the Boston small business owners. The place could be different: Boston, New York, Halifax, Philadelphia, London. Time and events could be altered: the Boston Tea Party; the Boston Massacre; the battle of Lexington and Concord. And the views could be changed. The remaining steps are then to select a set of choices among those; write a new stem; and put a key and plausible distractors with it.

Haladyna's approach has tons of advantages. Adapting an existing, successful item is a lot easier than writing an item from scratch. Once you identify the underlying structure and the variations on the keywords, writing several more items is relatively fast. Two other advantages are a little more subtle. Having to identify what the underlying structure is forces you to explore more deeply what each item is actually tapping, what the enacted learning objective actually is.

Another advantage is that if you do this enough, you may discover what some of the deep ideas or structures are in the courses you teach: the heuristics or templates which you're trying to teach your students. Olivia, for example, wants her students to understand that, regardless of the historical place or time, history is the interplay of how people and broader social movements influenced ideas and thus events. For her, the important things are not just the people, places and events, but why they happened and how they changed what people did and how they think. Olivia therefore uses this deep structure, of someone had a view of some event, often. Now that she knows that, she can bring this template explicitly to her students' attention and encourage them to use it.

With that deeper, foundational learning objective articulated and enacted in lots of questions on all her tests, she could conceivably "roll up" the results of all those items not only as evidence that her students understand the start of the American Revolution, and the US Senate's Golden Age, and the place and role of slavery throughout the period she's teaching, but also as evidence that they know how people and ideas interplay to influence events. Her department may well want to show some of these results as evidence for their outcomes assessment reports.

Using Item Analysis Information

Regardless of the method you use to generate parallel MCQs written to address the same learning objective, another check to determine if your items are indeed parallel is to look at the item analysis information after your questions have been piloted or used with a sufficient number of students (typically at least 30). Parallel items should have the same (or nearly the same) item difficulty and discrimination values. In Olivia's example above, if you discover that the item difficulty value for question 1A is 0.45 and for question 1B is 0.75 you would not use these as truly parallel items. It could be that identifying the impact of the Great Famine of Ireland is more difficult than identifying that the Great Famine of Ireland was the reason many Irish immigrants came to the United States. In that case, you might want to revise one of the questions and answer choices in some way.

Using Technology to Select and Deliver Item Pools

The previous sections on developing a test blueprint, writing MCQs, creating item shells, and conducting an item analysis all influence forming parallel MCQs. One of the advantages of creating item pools is that you can create parallel forms that have the overall same level of difficulty across all the questions on the form. There are a variety of software products that have a range of features to support creating and delivering MCQs in item banks. Table 8.1 provides an overview of these types of software, their advantages and disadvantages, and a few examples. The examples highlight some widely used products but are not exhaustive nor an endorsement of those products.

Table 8.1 Overview of Software for Creating MCQ Item Banks

Software category	Advantages	Disadvantages	Examples
Learning management systems (Dahlstrom et al., 2014)	Some include the ability to align learning objectives to an assessment or item bank. Integrated with the institution's gradebook system. Typically includes the ability to shuffle answer choice and/or question order. Some offer the ability to select questions from a question group or bank.	Not designed to be a sophisticated assessment system but rather support many features related to course and content delivery. Often learning objectives are aligned with the entire assessment (test, quiz) rather than to individual questions. Generally does not provide detailed item analysis information.	Blackboard Canvas Desire2Learn eCollege Moodle Sakai
Online quizzing software	Typically includes the ability to randomize parameters for numeric questions. Generally offers the ability to select questions from a question group or bank based on learning objective and/or difficulty.	As a third-party product, often requires some integration with the campus gradebook system.	ClassMarker EasyTestMaker ProProfs Quiz Maker QuizStar
High-stakes testing/ assessment software	Provides high level of security. Generally includes full item analysis reports.	Can be fairly expensive. As a third-party product, often requires some integration with the campus gradebook system.	ExamSoft Prometric Questionmark Respondus

Summary

Dr. Shah believes that creating an item bank is critical to the success of her course and plans to write three parallel multiple-choice questions for each of her learning objectives. Students will only get one attempt per quiz and exam so she thinks that using this strategy, as well as some other online administration strategies such as scrambling the order of her questions as well as answer choices, will help reduce any potential cheating concerns. While Dr. Shah knows how to use technology to address creating and administering MCQs online, she wonders what other technology features she can use to enhance her students' learning. In the next chapter, learn more about how technology can support giving students immediate feedback not only on the correctness of their MCQ answers, but also on the specific distractors they select.

References and Resources for Further Reading

Dahlstrom, E., Brooks, D. C., and Bichsel, J. (2014). *The Current Ecosystem of Learning Management Systems in Higher Education: Student, faculty, and IT perspectives. Research report*. Louisville, CO: ECAR, September 2014. Available from www.educause.edu/ecar.

Haladyna, T. M. (2004). *Developing and Validating Multiple-Choice Test Items*. Mahwah, NJ: Lawrence Erlbaum Associates.

Haladyna, T. M. and Shindoll, R. R. (1989). Item shells: A method for writing effective multiple-choice test items. *Evaluation & the Health Professions*, 12(1), 97–106.

9 The Power of Immediate Feedback

Imagine a situation where you've carefully crafted your multiple-choice questions with painstaking attention to writing an appropriate stem, creating distractors targeting common student misconceptions, and identifying the perfect correct answer that is attractive to the students who know the concept and not as attractive to those students who do not know the concept. The students take your assessment on a bubble sheet scantron, you take them to your campus scoring center after class, and within 24 hours the students receive an email with information about what questions they got right and wrong and you receive a report about how well the questions worked. In the next class, you enthusiastically prepare to go over multiple-choice questions ... only to realize the students are not really engaged; they might not recall why they selected an incorrect answer choice; and most of the comments from students are to argue why they should receive points for a wrong answer they think is correct. If this sounds familiar to you, there is still hope, lots of hope! In this chapter, we'll address feedback at the item level and in a subsequent chapter we'll talk more about broader strategies you can employ to increase the learning for your students after the test.

Online technologies can not only deliver assessments that have graphics, audio, and video but can also provide immediate feedback as students work through a MCQ assessment or after they complete one. This assessment can be done during or outside of class for either low-stakes or high-stakes situations. This feedback can range from a focus on misconceptions targeted at specific answer choices to overall performance for individual students or the entire class. We'll demonstrate how to write effective feedback for MCQs and how to leverage the technology to support feedback to students to improve their learning.

Targeted and Timely Feedback

Feedback refers to information given to students about a performance, response, or action that they can use to guide their learning and/or improve their next performance. In a MCQ, *targeted* feedback informs students about what they are or are not understanding in the choice they selected and gives guidance about how to remediate their error if they answered incorrectly. In a MCQ, this feedback should address the misconception embedded in the distractors for the incorrect answers and reinforce the concept being addressed in the correct answer. Feedback aimed at correcting errors and misconceptions should also be *timely* and occur immediately after a response is given if the MCQ is being used for formative assessment. In this situation, the focus of the immediate feedback is to support students' subsequent practice on a particular concept or learning objective. Research shows that timely and targeted feedback can significantly enhance student performance by addressing misconceptions as students have them (Butler and Winne, 1995; Corbett and Anderson, 2001; Hattie and Timperley, 2007; National Research Council, 2000; Wiggins, 1998). In general, more frequent feedback given immediately after a student responds to a MCQ is better. However, the timing and frequency of feedback should align with your learning goals for the activity or assessment in which you are using MCQs (see Hattie and Timperley (2007) for a discussion of timing issues).

The goal of instructional feedback is to help students decrease the distance between what they understand about a specific task and what you hope they understood. Task-specific feedback focuses on the particular answer choice to a problem that the student selects and how that choice is reflective of the student's level of understanding. This feedback can direct the student about what needs to be revised, or provide suggestions to assist the student in making her own revisions (Shute, 2008). Task-specific feedback has its greatest impact on student learning when it informs students about their progress and/or provides suggestions to them about how to proceed. One way to fill this gap is to explicitly let students know if their answer is correct or incorrect, and supplement that with specific directions or alternative strategies for understanding the information. These directions may focus on redirecting students to more or different information they need to answer the question correctly. However, feedback on the task is more powerful when students have misconceptions rather than when they lack the necessary information on how to answer a question (Hattie and Timperley, 2007). For students who do not have the necessary background knowledge to answer a question, feedback may not be helpful in addressing their knowledge gap.

It can be challenging to write not only the question, correct answer, and distractors, but also the corresponding feedback for each response choice, but if you have the technology to deliver online assessments the value in immediate feedback will pay long-term dividends for you and your students. Figure 9.1 shows an example from Dr. Shah's introductory statistics course.

Hattie (1999) conducted a meta-analysis exploring the most effective types of feedback. The most effective forms of feedback have the following characteristics: they provide cues or reinforcement to students, are in video-, audio-, or computer-assisted formats, and relate to specific learning goals.

Given the data below, which of the following represents the median?

    7 2 5 6 3 7 9 8 1

    a) 3
    b) 5
    c) 6
    d) 7

Feedback

    a) Incorrect. To determine the median you first need to order your data from the smallest to the largest value. It appears that you forgot to order the data set as the middle number in this unordered data set is 3.

    b) Incorrect. The mean is the arithmetic average of the data set, or the sum of the numbers divided by N, the total number of values. It appears you calculated the mean (48/9 = 5.33 ~ 5) instead of the median.

    c) Correct. The median is the middle number in a data set ordered from the smallest to the largest value. In this case, the median is six: 1, 2, 3, 5, **6**, 7, 7, 8, 9.

    d) Incorrect. It appears you confused the median with the mode, which is the most frequently occurring number. For this data set, the mode is 7.

Figure 9.1 Example Statistics MCQ with Feedback

Praise (e.g. "Good job!", "Well done!", "Excellent!") was one of the least effective forms of feedback in enhancing achievement (Hattie, 1999). Feedback is most beneficial when it helps students address misconceptions and provides cues to the appropriate strategies to use to answer a question (Hattie and Timperley, 2007). Feedback that lacks in specificity may cause students to view it as useless, or even worse, become frustrated (Shute, 2008).

There is no one format for writing targeted feedback for MCQs, but there are some general guidelines you can follow. First, indicate whether the answer choice is correct or incorrect before each explanation, known as verification. In some cases, it may even be appropriate to use something like "Not quite right" for answer choices that are partially correct but not the best option.

After verifying whether or not the answer choice selected is correct, you should provide an explanation that targets the student's specific response. Response-specific feedback appears to enhance student learning efficiency more than other types of feedback (Corbett and Anderson, 2001). The explanation should address the student misconception(s) in the incorrect answer choices. The feedback for the incorrect answers should be written to target the misconceptions that are appropriate for the level of the student (e.g. lower division undergraduate, upper division undergraduate, graduate) and should be based on the instructor's experience of the common mistakes students make. Also, feedback should provide some guidance to the student about how to arrive at the correct answer. Lastly, feedback for the key, or correct answer, should reinforce why the answer is correct rather than simply state, "Correct" or "Great job!" Since one of the drawbacks of multiple-choice questions is that students are able to guess, feedback should provide a reason why that selection is correct for students who may have selected that answer by chance. Even if they knew it was the right answer, they may not know why it's the right answer. They may not have remembered all of the aspects of what makes it the right answer. And, to return to our formative assessment cycle, this is one more opportunity to have the cycle revolve one more time.

While research has demonstrated the positive effect of response-specific feedback on enhancing student learning, results are inconclusive as to the appropriate length and complexity for feedback. With distractors, we suggest providing enough detail to address the misconceptions and providing some strategies for how to arrive at the correct answer. With keys, we suggest providing reinforcing information about why the choice is correct. Revisiting the example parallel math questions from Chapter 8, you can see how the feedback is written to address the underlying misconception but is tailored to the specific values in each version (Figure 9.2).

Another aspect of how students attend to and use the feedback is whether it is actually "score justification" or whether it is truly feedback that will impact their next performance. The key issue which makes the difference is whether there is an explicit opportunity for students to benefit from an increase in their learning or not. If there is no explicit opportunity for them to benefit from the feedback, they may not choose to look at it at all, and if they do, they will do so to have their score justified ("Why did I miss that question?"), but rarely for the purely intrinsic reasons (e.g. "What can I learn from this?"). Even the most intrinsically motivated learners make cost-benefit decisions about what to do with their time. While a grade must be recorded at some point, and you've only got so much time and attention to be revising scores, there are some strategies you could consider for providing these explicit opportunities for them to benefit from the feedback. Briefly here, you could employ a cumulative final examination so that the feedback on mid-term exams would be relevant to the final. With the technology and item banks, you could also let students retake quizzes, for example, once or even twice. We discuss some other, broader ways to provide "next opportunities" in Chapter 13.

In working with instructors, Dawn has found that asking them to write feedback can be a very powerful activity in their own learning process. A distractor that made so much sense when writing the question no longer seems clear when having to write feedback about its underlying misconception. Writing feedback also challenges you to think about *why* a student might select a particular distractor and how you can use the MCQ to diagnose your students' knowledge gaps. The process of writing feedback not only benefits your students during and after the assessment itself, but it is an effective tool as you construct your MCQs to help you make explicit the learning you are trying to assess.

Student A: What is the appropriate value of 'x' when solving the following equation?

2x + 3 = 7

a) –2
b) 2
c) 5
d) 8

Student B: What is the appropriate value of 'x' when solving the following equation?

3x + 1 = 7

a) –2
b) 2
c) 2 2/3
d) 18

Feedback for Student A

a) Incorrect. It appears you may have subtracted 7 from 3 (3 – 7) instead of subtracting 3 from 7 (7 – 3) when isolating the X variable term in the first step in solving this problem.

b) Correct! The process for solving this equation is to 1) isolate the X variable term on one side of the equation: 2x + 3 – 3 = 7 – 3 or 2x = 4; and then 2) divide by the constant associated with the X variable: 2x/2 = 4/2 or 1x = 2 giving the final answer of X = 2.

c) Incorrect. It appears you may have added 3 to 7 (7 + 3) instead of subtracting 3 from 7 (7 – 3) when isolating the X variable term in the first step in solving this problem.

d) Incorrect. It appears that you correctly subtracted 3 from 7 (7 – 3) when isolating the X variable term in the first step in solving this problem to get 2x = 4 but multiplied both sides by 2 (2x * 2 = 4 * 2) instead of dividing by 2 (2x/2 = 4/2) in the second step.

Feedback for Student B

a) Incorrect. It appears you may have subtracted 7 from 1 (1 – 7) instead of subtracting 1 from 7 (7 – 1) when isolating the X variable term in the first step in solving this problem.

b) Correct! The process for solving this equation is to 1) isolate the X variable term on one side of the equation: 3x + 1 – 1 = 7 – 1 or 3x = 6; and then 2) divide by the number associated with the X variable: 3x/3 = 6/3 or 1x = 2 giving the final answer of X = 2.

c) Incorrect. It appears you may have added 1 to 7 (7 + 1) instead of subtracting 1 from 7 (7 – 1) when isolating the X variable term in the first step in solving this problem.

d) Incorrect. It appears that you correctly subtracted 3 from 7 (7 – 3) when isolating the X variable term in the first step in solving this problem to get 2x = 4 but multiplied both sides by 3 (3x * 3 = 6 * 3) instead of dividing by 3 (3x/3 = 6/2) in the second step.

Figure 9.2 Example Parallel Math MCQs with Feedback

When to Give Feedback

Various learning management systems and other products allow you to specify when and how students receive this feedback. You can specify that students see the feedback after each question response so that they can immediately address their misconception and try again. If you prefer, you can have students answer all of the questions at once and then receive feedback on the collective set of MCQs. Research on feedback and timing suggests that the timing of feedback is dependent on the nature of the task and the ability of the learner (Mathan and Koedinger, 2002).

The ways in which you vary how feedback is presented should be aligned with your instructional objectives for the assessment. If you want students to engage with the material and reply to the assessment for the purpose of scaffolding their learning with little or no grade associated with the assessment, then you would provide students with immediate feedback after each response and the ability to answer the question as many times as they wish until they get the question correct. If you want more of a snapshot of their understanding you may wish to set up the assessment so that feedback is provided immediately after answering the entire set of MCQs. The latter would be a more traditional online quiz which could be taken inside or outside of class, depending on the weight and stakes of the assessment.

Data-Based Decision-Making

In addition to being able to receive immediate feedback about specific questions, educational technologies can provide students with data about their individual performance as well as that of the class as a whole. Learning dashboards often enable students to track their individual performance on MCQs for a particular assessment or across assessments. Multiple-choice questions tied to learning outcomes can offer students information about their progress toward mastery of the material. This feedback can empower students to take ownership of their own learning.

Student feedback about individual misconceptions on a MCQ or performance across one or more assessments can also be complemented by data about the performance of the class as a whole. Students who not only receive feedback about their own performance but can view aggregate information about how other students in the class are performing on an individual MCQ or across a set of questions are given the opportunity to compare their own learning against other students in the class. We know that students are typically poor at estimating their own understanding in that students who do know a concept tend to underestimate their learning and students who do not know the concept tend to overestimate their learning (Kruger and Dunning, 1999; Kennedy et al., 2002). Comparison data can help mediate this effect so that students are able to measure their own learning against the group as a whole and seek additional support if they realize they are not on par with their peers.

However, some studies suggest comparative feedback can negatively impact learning and motivation. When feedback compares a student's performance with that of others, poor performers tend to attribute their failures to lack of ability, expect to perform poorly in the future, and demonstrate decreased motivation on subsequent tasks. Self-referenced feedback that compares performance with other measures of a student's ability is generally preferable to feedback that compares a student's performance with others, particularly for low-achieving students (Shute, 2008). Further, encouraging students to compare themselves to others decreases the emphasis on individual mastery (i.e. learning) of the learning objectives. Jay usually refuses to report the class mean and standard deviation on exams, which is, at first, wildly unpopular. He explains, though, that each student needs to be concerned about how well he mastered the material. If he is content or unhappy about his own score, it does not matter how everyone else did. If the mean was low, that is an instructor issue and not a learner issue.

In addition to student feedback, feedback information about student performance on your MCQs is valuable for you as the instructor of the course. Warning systems built into LMS, such as Purdue University's *Course Signals* (www.itap.purdue.edu/studio/signals/), can give you information about how individual students and the class as a whole are performing on your MCQs. You may discover that most of the class are struggling on a particular concept and you need to provide some more instruction on this topic. Warning systems can also provide the opportunity for you to suggest some instructional interventions for those students who are struggling with specific concepts by building suggestions into the feedback.

Summary

Feedback can be a very effective tool to support students' learning, particularly when combined with the power of technology. With multiple-choice questions, the ability to directly target students' misconceptions and provide immediate, targeted feedback on the task as they respond to questions has been shown to be an invaluable aid to the learning process. Navigating how and when question-level feedback is complemented by feedback about the student's progress toward meeting various learning objectives, in comparison with their peers, and to provide alerts to you and the students, can be a tricky process. The type, nature, and frequency with which you give feedback to your students will depend on your comfort level in creating and using the feedback as well as the ability of your students to use the feedback to support their learning.

Up until this point, we have focused on using technology to create, administer, and provide feedback in online MCQ assessments that students typically take outside of the classroom. In the next chapter, we will explore several strategies for integrating technology-enhanced MCQs into your classroom activities.

References and Resources for Further Reading

Butler, D. L. and Winne, P. H. (1995). Feedback and self-regulated learning: A theoretical synthesis. *Review of Educational Research*, 65(3), 245–81.

Corbett, A. T. and Anderson, J. R. (2001). Locus of feedback control in computer-based tutoring: Impact on learning rate, achievement and attitudes. *Proceedings of ACM CHI 2001 Conference on Human Factors in Computing Systems*, 245–52.

Hattie, J. A. (1999, August). Influences on student learning. Inaugural Lecture, University of Auckland, New Zealand. Retrieved April 22, 2015 from http://growthmindseteaz.org/files/Influencesonstudent2C683_1_.pdf

Hattie, J. and Timperley, H. (2007). The power of feedback. *Review of Educational Research*, 77(1), 81–112.

Kennedy, E. J., Lawton, L., and Plumlee, E. L. (2002). Blissful ignorance: The problem of unrecognized incompetence and academic performance. *Journal of Marketing Education*, 24(3), 243–52.

Kruger, J. and Dunning, D. (1999). Unskilled and unaware of it: How difficulties in recognizing one's own incompetence lead to inflated self-assessments. *Journal of Personality and Social Psychology*, 77(6), 1121–34.

Mathan, S. A. and Koedinger, K. R. (2002). An empirical assessment of comprehension fostering features in an intelligent tutoring system. In S. A. Cerri, G. Gouarderes, and F. Paraguacu (eds.) *Intelligent Tutoring Systems*, 6th International Conference, ITS 2002 (Vol. 2363, pp. 330–43). New York: Springer-Verlag.

National Research Council. (2000). *How People Learn: Brain, Mind, Experience, and School: Expanded Edition*. Washington, DC: National Academies Press.

Sandeen, C. (2013). Assessment's place in the new MOOC world. *Research & Practice in Assessment*, 8(2), 5–12.

Shute, V. J. (2008). Focus on formative feedback. *Review of Educational Research*, 78(1), 153–89.

Wiggins, G. (1998). *Educative Assessment: Designing Assessments to Inform and Improve Student Performance*. San Francisco: Jossey-Bass.

10 Technology in the Classroom

While technology is often used to deliver assessments outside of the classroom, there are several ways in which technology can support in-class delivery of MCQs. We will explore student response systems, also called "clickers", and how to write effective multiple-choice "clicker questions" to elicit the in-class student learning you want to reinforce. We will also discuss other technology solutions that use MCQs to support in-class learning and assessment.

Clickers and MCQs

Student response systems, also known as classroom response systems, audience response systems, electronic response systems, and more generally "clickers", gained popularity in college classrooms starting in the early 2000s. In these systems, instructors would pose a question verbally, by typing it "on the fly" into the software system, or in a pre-planned presentation displayed to students. Students used a physical device to respond to questions, typically in multiple-choice format, with the press of a button. Those responses were recorded by a receiver and summarized by a software system running off a computer workstation. Instructors could immediately display aggregate results, typically in the form of a histogram of the answer choices selected to the entire class to provide immediate feedback to students and/or as a genesis for a discussion on the question. Responses could be collected anonymously or recorded in a database for purposes such as assigning class participation grades and taking attendance.

Today, some clicker systems allow students to use their smartphone, tablet, or other mobile device in lieu of the student or institution purchasing individual response devices. Some systems can now collect alphanumeric input to allow for numeric and short-answer student responses.

Research shows that using clickers leads to greater class participation compared to some non-technology solutions such as raising hands or holding up response cards (Stowell and Nelson, 2007). Additionally, students in classes that use clickers score higher on exams than students in classes that do not use clickers (Freeman *et al.*, 2007; Morling *et al.*, 2008). Given that such systems meet our definition of a revolution of the formative assessment cycle, we're not surprised!

Sam Oliver recently learned of a clicker system supported by his institution and decided to give it a try. Since his biology class increased from 20 to 50 students in each section he's now teaching, he had to drop the reading journals he previously used. By using clickers he can still have students do the reading assignments and can use in-class clickers as a way to evaluate their understanding of the reading assignments at the start of every class. Sam realizes this might help him to identify the concepts students are able to get on their own from the assigned readings so that he can focus his class activities on working with students to apply and synthesize the critical biology concepts.

Writing MCQs for clicker questions should follow the same principles outlined in preceding chapters of this book. The question stems should focus on high-level concepts and the distractors should contain common student misconceptions. However, you may need to adjust the question difficulty based on whether you are using the in-class MCQ clicker questions to assess concepts you have yet to discuss in class (like Sam's reading assignments) or at the end of a unit of instruction.

Prior to a lesson, you might expect students to gain a surface-level understanding of the concepts through reading assignments or working through online modules. In that case, you might want to use the clicker questions to determine the concepts with which students are most struggling. You can then tailor your classroom instruction and activities to target the concepts that are most challenging for students. At the end of a lesson, you might expect students to have a deeper understanding of the concepts and could use clicker questions as a "knowledge check" of sorts before having them engage in a high-stakes MCQ assessment such as a quiz or exam. You could use these end-of-lesson clicker questions to tailor review sessions and/or provide students with information about the concepts that they have yet to master. Whether using in-class clicker questions at the beginning, middle, or end of a lesson, you want to model the types of MCQs students will see in their higher-stakes assessment during these lower-stakes, formative assessment opportunities.

Team-Based Learning

While clickers have been a useful technology to pair with administering low-stakes multiple-choice assessments, another approach to using MCQs during in-class instruction is team-based learning. Team-based learning originated with Larry Michaelson in the 1970s. Team-based learning is an instructional strategy that supports the development of high-performance learning teams and provides opportunities for these teams to engage in meaningful learning activities.

- Instructors place students into permanent small groups of five to seven students, called learning teams.
- Before receiving instruction on a topic, students do the reading assignment for a class that uses a textbook or works through online materials (for example, in a flipped classroom format) for the unit with the goal to acquire a broad understanding of the topic.
- In class, the students engage in the Readiness Assurance Process (RAP). Individually, students take a short quiz, typically in multiple-choice form, on the reading assignment. Once all students have turned in the quiz, the students take the same quiz in their learning teams. The team quizzes are completed on scratch-off forms that show the correct answer. Both the individual and team quizzes count as part of the course grade.
- After the RAP phase, groups are allowed to engage in an appeals process whereby they can submit a written appeal if they believe their answer should be counted as correct and why.
- Based on the performance of the teams, the instructor provides corrective instruction tailored to the questions that most groups did not get correct. The instructor uses subsequent classes to provide more in-depth instruction, application activities during class and as homework.
- This process is repeated for each new topic with students remaining in the same learning team throughout the course (Fink, 2002).

The multiple-choice individual and team quizzes are a critical component of the team-based learning process. Unlike summative assessments, MCQs used in the RAP should address key concepts from the readings, but avoid focusing on overly detailed information. Additionally, the questions should focus on foundational concepts but be challenging enough to promote discussion within the teams (Michaelson, 2002). We discuss other similar kinds of activities in Chapters 12 and 13.

Writing MCQs for team-based learning quizzes follows the same general principles we have been outlining throughout this book. The primary consideration you want to keep in mind is that students have not yet had any formal instruction in the topic and their learning is based on reading assignments or online modules in which they learn surface-level concepts. Therefore, the questions should aim at learning objectives the students should be able to learn on their own by engaging with resources materials for the course.

Dawn used a team-based learning approach in teaching her introductory statistics course with approximately 100 students. Figure 10.1 shows an example of one of her RAP quiz questions and its corresponding item analysis information.

A negatively skewed distribution of scores with a mean of 50 and a standard deviation of 10 has been transformed into z-scores. Which of the following is correct about the distribution of z-scores?

 a) The z-score distribution will have a mean of 0 and a standard deviation of 1.**
 b) The z-score distribution will have a mean of 0 and a standard deviation of -1.
 c) The z-score distribution will have a mean of 5 and a standard deviation of 10.
 d) The z-score distribution will have the same mean and standard deviation as
    the original distribution.
 e) The distribution of z-scores will have a normally shaped distribution.

Item analysis information:

Difficulty = 0.62, Discrimination = 0.64

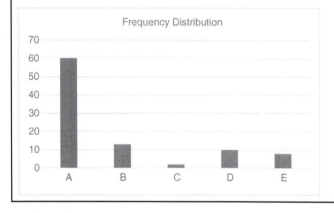

Figure 10.1 Example Readiness Assurance Process MCQ and Corresponding Item
         Analysis Information

In this sample question, some students have a misconception that a negatively skewed distribution has a negative standard deviation – and that the standard deviation can be less than 0 (option B)! A similar number of students incorrectly interpreted the z-score transformation to have exactly the same mean and standard deviation as its original distribution (option C). You can immediately address these misconceptions after students complete the Readiness Assurance Process team quizzes if several of the teams also get this item incorrect.

You might be wondering, why all the focus on team-based learning in a section on technology in the classroom? Well, just as clickers can be used to conduct formative assessments in the classroom, they can also be used to facilitate the team-based learning process. The primary difference is that students would not be shown the answers or distribution of responses during their individual quiz portion. Also, the system would have to be set up to track responses rather than allow for anonymous answers, since including some portion of the individual and team quizzes toward a course grade is an essential part of team-based learning. Lastly, the system would need to be set up to display correct answers to all the questions on the quiz after all the teams have answered the quiz, not after each question, as is typically the case with clicker systems.

Peer-Learning Technologies

An extension of both clicker systems and team-based learning is a classroom-based peer-instruction technology called Learning Catalytics (https://learningcatalytics.com/). Similar to clicker systems and team-based learning, students individually respond to questions. The system supports any web-enabled device to respond to questions. If you have populated the system with a seat map of the classroom, the system can automatically assign students to groups to engage in peer-to-peer instruction. You determine the parameters for group assignments such as group size, correctness of the response, and location in the room. The students then discuss the question or set of questions with their peers and can resubmit their answers. This system supports not only multiple-choice questions but also a variety of question formats.

When writing MCQs for a system like Learning Catalytics, the emphasis is on asking questions that will reveal common misconceptions students have about the material. Additionally, the question should be moderately difficult, with about 30 to 70 percent of the students answering the question correctly before peer discussion (Learning Catalytics, 2015).

Summary

Integrating technology-enhanced solutions in the classroom was once a timely and costly endeavor. Students are increasingly connected to their technology devices and you can now easily leverage the power of these devices to provide students frequent assessment opportunities during class. This allows you to keep abreast of your students' learning while also keeping them engaged. Clickers, team-based learning technologies, and peer learning systems have evolved to integrate the power of technology with research on learning to support and enhance both your and your students' experiences in the classroom. MCQs embedded in these class-room technology systems are an excellent vehicle to quickly assess and provide feedback to your students about their learning as it is happening in the classroom.

References and Resources for Further Reading

Freeman, S., O'Connor, E., Parks, J. W., Cunningham, M., Hurley, D., and Haak, D. (2007). Prescribed active learning increases performance in introductory biology. *CBE-Life Sciences Education*, 6, 132–9.

Fink, L. D. (2002). Beyond small groups: Harnessing the extraordinary power of learning teams. In L. K. Michaelson, A. B. Knight, and L. D. Fink (eds.) *Team-Based Learning: A transformative use of small groups*. Westport, CT: Praeger.

Learning Catalytics (2015). *Designing good questions to ask*. Retrieved May 25, 2015 from the Learning Catalytics Instructor Help website: http://help.pearsoncmg.com/learning_catalytics/instructor/en/index.htm#Topics/lc_design_good_questions.htm

Michaelson, L. K. (2002). Getting started with team-based learning. In L. K. Michaelson, A. B. Knight, and L. D. Fink (eds.) *Team-Based Learning: A transformative use of small groups*. Westport, CT: Praeger.

Morling, B., McAuliffe, M., Cohen, L., and D'Lorenzo, T. (2008). Efficacy of personal response systems ("clickers") in large, introductory psychology classes. *Teaching of Psychology*, 35, 45–50.

Stowell, J. R. and Nelson, J. M. (2007). Benefits of electronic audience response systems on student participation, learning, and emotion. *Teaching of Psychology*, 34, 253–8.

Section IV

Teaching and Learning through Multiple-Choice Questions

11 Before the Test

There are a great many ways in which you and your students can leverage an upcoming multiple-choice test to maximize their learning. Some of them are tried-and-true methods like a study guide and practice tests or questions, and others are less well known, like studying from the test blueprint. We'll start down a list of tactics in just a moment. We would like to begin, though, by discussing some key principles that sway our thinking about promoting learning in college classrooms, and that we hope will sway yours, too. One, which has already been discussed at least twice so far in this book, is the formative assessment cycle; another is leveraging existing activities; and a third is scaffolding.

Let's return to the formative assessment cycle from Chapter 1 (see Figure 11.1). You'll recall that learning is maximized when all three parts of the cycle occur so that the cycle spins at a rate measured in rps (revolutions per semester). The more rps, the more learning. Even before the test, we want this cycle revolving, which means we need to create or identify assessment events prior to the test and feedback prior to the test.

Often when we say "assessment event", college instructors think "gradebook entry", but that's actually only a subset of assessment events. Not every assessment must be graded. (This could be a real conceptual shift for you and your students, so, if you need to pause to absorb that, we'll understand.) If you're going to focus on maximizing student learning (as opposed to maximizing student grades) and you're going to encourage your students to focus on learning, not on grades, the first thing you need to do is to uncouple the concepts of assessment and grading in your and your students' thinking. There are plenty of assessment events which don't "count" toward the grade. (But they do count; that is, they are important in advancing learning!) You need to value opportunities for students to receive feedback on their learning as often as possible from as many sources as possible, and then you need to help students value that, too.

In order to do that, there's a second deconstruction which needs to occur: you need to uncouple yourself from feedback. Many college instructors mistakenly assume that they are the only viable, credible source of

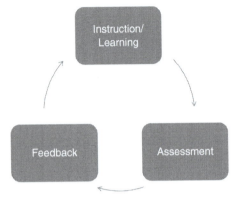

Figure 11.1 The Formative Assessment Cycle

feedback for students. We heard you groan a moment ago when we said students need lots of feedback! You groaned because you think you, then, need to be directly responsible for all of that extra feedback. We're delighted to tell you that you've got lots of help, and that's even if you're not fortunate enough to have a teaching assistant. Your students are surrounded by sources of feedback: the textbook, the internet, each other, themselves and you. Even if we're talking about your being the source of feedback, there are lots of ways that can be asynchronous. Chapter 9 on immediate feedback has tons of examples. Any resource you prepare and give to students can be a source of feedback to them whether feedback was the primary purpose or a secondary or tertiary purpose. Perhaps a few examples would help.

Preet's online course could include a FACQ (frequently asked content questions) section where she answers common *content* questions. (She has a FAPPQ, too, where PP is for "process and procedures" about non-content issues like due dates.) Over time, she could build this up so that it truly did address frequently asked content questions. Then she needs to encourage students to use it. She has a "submit a question" form in her learning management software so students can ask her (instead of emailing her). When students click on that link, there's a short form there that includes several checkboxes: "Did you look at the FACQ for an answer to your question?"; "Did you ask a classmate for an answer to your question?"; "Did you look in the textbook?"; "Did you look in the course resources?"; followed by: "If you answered yes to all of those and you still don't have an answer to your question, please type your question in the field below and click the submit button." This technique encourages students to consider multiple resources other than Preet to get help or feedback while still making Preet available. It also cuts down drastically on the number of questions she gets. Preet has constructed and/or provided all of those resources, so students should be encouraged to use them.

Sam encourages students to use the practice quizzes the textbook provides at the end of each chapter. Since a key is provided, students can check their own answers. It's an oldie but a goodie as an example of a student self-managed formative assessment cycle.

Olivia has students write their own multiple-choice questions as a study exercise and then share them with peers. The peers provide correction and feedback on the items.

The second principle we will work with is leveraging existing activities. Adding more things for your students to do is not always the best answer to increasing the rps of the formative assessment cycle. More efficient, and sometimes even more effective, is enhancing or augmenting existing activities to get additional assessment and/or feedback.

For example, Sam had a teaching assistant prepare explanations for the answers to the end-of-chapter questions so that students don't just receive right/wrong feedback, but receive an explanation for why B is correct and A, C, and D are not. Olivia always takes attendance in her class sessions, for which she used to use the clicker attendance function. Now she has one or two MCQs projected as students are walking into class, which they need to answer. Early in the semester, she immediately talks about them so that responding to them has explicit value for the students. Later in the semester she sometimes launches into the day's lesson without referring to them.

The third principle is scaffolding. No, we're not encouraging you to think about assessment like an executioner! That is antithetical to our philosophy. Scaffolding is a cognitive psychology principle for learning that says learners need more explicit support and guidance (i.e. scaffolds) in their early learning and then the scaffolding can be gradually removed until students' learning is self-supporting. Olivia is scaffolding her students by explicitly discussing her MCQ attendance-taking early in the semester and then letting it go without discussion at times later in the semester.

With those three principles in mind – making the formative assessment cycle spin, leveraging existing activities, and scaffolding – we can now examine a menu of possible activities you and your students can engage in before they take the test.

Generic Assessment Information

That first day of class is so important! It sets a tone for your entire term together, signals immediately what is valued in the course, and accomplishes much "housekeeping". When you're talking with them about assessment and grading in the course, we strongly encourage you to go beyond the housekeeping of describing what kinds of assessments there will be, how many points each will be worth, and your policies on late assignments and accommodating disabilities. Using our principle of leveraging existing activities – because you're covering those issues anyway – and our focus on student learning, use this time to communicate some of the substance of those decisions. For example, Sam has a "no late work" policy without exception. He does this, though, because he knows that environmental engineers must have contract bids in by the advertised deadline or they will not be considered for the contract. In other words, meeting hard deadlines is a professional skill for the students in his courses. Better to lose an A for a B in the course because of a late assignment and learn that lesson now than to lose a contract and possibly one's job two years from now.

It's perfectly acceptable, and perhaps even advisable, also to share some of the pragmatic reasons for your assessments, assessment choices, and assessment policies. Olivia's department chair has tasked her with producing the outcomes assessment data from her course to show student progress against the community college's institution-wide, general student learning outcomes for the upcoming institutional accreditation visit. Olivia can and should mention that to her students.

At any time, though, and especially on the first day of class, we urge you to make explicit connections for students back to their own learning. How do all of these aspects contribute to student learning, and what implications do these aspects have for what students should do and focus on in class?

Studying (for the Test)

A learning-oriented student will be doing lots of things outside of class to be ready for in-class time – you know, that old rule that students should spend three hours outside of class for each hour they spend in class. They will be doing something related to your course every day. What they are doing will depend, in part, on what you suggest or require for that time and on what is happening in the course. Should they be working on an upcoming paper or other assignment? Should they be reading the textbook? And so on.

Grade-oriented students will be doing things outside of class, too, but their focus is on test preparation and completing graded work. They tend not to do optional assignments (unless there's extra credit) or ungraded work.

Since you're trying to promote learning and foster learning-oriented students, you want to aid students to do the former kinds of studying and not the latter. You want students to understand that anything they do that deepens or betters their own learning in the course *is* test preparation. Several things you do will implicitly and explicitly communicate this message. Students quickly sniff out inconsistencies and will label you a hypocrite. Essentially, you want the answers to these two questions to be identical: "What is important in class?" and "What will be on the test?" Here's how to avoid those inconsistencies. First, you've got clear learning objectives or student learning outcomes for your course. As we've already discussed, this gives you explicit and clear answers to both those questions. Second, you've got your test blueprint that you're using both for instructional planning and assessment planning, which provides the linchpin which holds instruction and assessment together. Third, you now are able to address the connections with students in all of your communications with them.

To summarize, in order to foster learning-oriented students, studying and preparing for each day of class should be studying for the test. Studying for the test should not be terribly different from studying in general. And, with your instruction and assessment well aligned to learning objectives, studying for the test is not a detour or sidetrack to learning but promotes learning.

Using the Test Blueprint

In Chapter 4, we introduced the idea of giving your test blueprint to students well ahead of time, using it with them in class, and encouraging them to use it themselves.

Giving students the test blueprint for a chunk of your course gives you the opportunity to share important professional information with them, as we've said. When you start a new unit or section of the course, one great way to promote learning is to provide an advanced organizer to students – a road-map, if you will – of where they will be going and what they will be seeing in this section of the course. A test blueprint is an awesome advanced organizer. It quickly captures for them what the major topics are and how you will expect them to know those topics. This discussion with them could include some example questions (perhaps even test questions) or situations that illustrate the different cells in the table.

In class, then, as you move from topic to topic, or sometimes cell to cell, refer explicitly to the test blueprint and perhaps to the example questions or situations. Can we answer this question now? This should be scaffolded so that you're doing this very explicitly and intentionally early in the semester and transitioning students to doing it themselves later in the term.

You also want to encourage students to use the blueprint, too, to guide their studying. How much time and/or energy should they be spending on different topics? Since the blueprint proportions instructional time and testing real estate, it also should help students apportion their studying efforts.

Practice Makes Perfect

Students need lots of opportunities to practice the skills and to use the knowledge represented in the learning objectives. There are lots of options here, like the questions or exercises at the end of chapters; practice tests, etc., on your textbook publisher's website; worked examples that you give to students. These can take lots of forms and are beyond the scope of this book.

One approach that does explicitly employ MCQs is having students write MCQs about course content as a study strategy and perhaps for inclusion on the "live" exam itself. Whether and how you wish to do this with your students involves some cost-benefit analysis (e.g. Bates *et al.*, 2014; Fellenz, 2004). There is definitely benefit: studies have shown that students who write test questions as a study strategy do better on the test than students who do not write test questions (e.g. Foos, 1989; Kerkman *et al.*, 1994). You can ask students not only to write MCQs but also to write explanations of options (why they're right or wrong) or broader explanations about solution strategies, for example. There are also some costs: you do need to spend some time to make sure students understand good item-writing technique and different ways of knowing. You could have students employ the test blueprint for their item-writing. With some training, students are able to write quality MCQs (e.g. Bates *et al.*, 2014).

It is also possible to employ software such as PeerWise (https://peerwise. cs.auckland.ac.nz/) to reduce the administrative burden on instructors and to engage peers. Engaging peers is a great way to provide feedback to students, thus upping the rps rate of the formative assessment cycle.

If you're going to use student-constructed MCQs in the "live" exam, you'll want to make sure that you're reviewing them for quality and fitting them into your blueprint. You may also wish to reduce the impact that students' familiarity with those items might have on the exam score by making sure there's a large pool of student-generated items to choose from and/or making them a relatively small portion of the total "live" items on the test.

The "cheat sheet", while not specific to MCQs, is one we often end up talking with instructors about. Here, we are referring to asking students to prepare a "sheet" of notes which they will be allowed to use during the exam itself. This is not "open book – open notes" but rather a single sheet. Jay, for example, permits students to bring "one 8½ x 11 inch double-sided sheet of notes; any size font but no magnifying glass" to exams. On the other hand, Dawn prepares the "cheat sheet" for her students which includes relevant formulas and definitions that students need to know how to apply, to ensure that all students have the same resource materials during her exams. There are several rationales. First, preparing the cheat sheet is itself a study activity. Second, having the sheet seems to reduce student anxiety during the test. Third, if you're writing strong, conceptual questions, having a cheat sheet should not actually be providing students with answers. (See Erbe (2007) for more details on crib sheets.)

Preparing for the Test

While it aids learning and a learning orientation to have studying and studying for the test be as similar as possible, there really are distinct test preparation activities for you and your students.

You have an obligation to articulate clearly for your students what will be on the test well in advance of the test, so that your students can be well prepared. This is a validity concern and a cognitive load concern for the test itself. If students aren't fully aware of what to expect on the test, they likely won't be well prepared, and then the students won't show what they actually know on the test. When students are surprised during the test, by content or formats they weren't expecting, it heightens their anxiety and other emotions (e.g. fear, anger, frustration), which take up cognitive bandwidth.

You need to communicate early and often with students about issues like how much time they will have for the test; what item formats will be on the test; if they may consult resources, and if so, which resources; what materials they will need and be allowed to use (e.g. scratch paper, note sheets; number 2 pencils, calculators, etc.). This information can be scaffolded throughout the semester, being more explicit and detailed early, and less so later in the term.

It is often useful, especially for the first exam of the semester, to provide example items to students. If you're using particular variants like vignette-based items, context-dependent item sets, or binary choice, you'll want to make sure they know how those formats work. You can do this in lots of ways, including using the formats during class activities and including them in practice tests or study guides.

Occasionally, we hear college instructors object to teaching study skills and/or test-taking skills. There are some factors that definitely should contribute to how and how much of that you "should" be doing, or rather, how much of those skills you expect your students to have already. The academic level of your students is a large factor. Junior undergraduates are going to have more studying and test-taking experience than first-year college students will (and more bad habits!). In our experience, though, assuming graduate students have these skills can be risky because so many of them are years away from their undergraduate work. We've often heard graduate students say, "I haven't taken a multiple choice test in 20 years!" Another factor is, regardless of their academic level, whether they actually have these skills or not. Sometimes you will encounter students who simply don't yet have good test-preparation and good test-taking skills. So whether they *should* have them already and whether someone else *should* have taught them doesn't change the fact that they don't, and you have the opportunity to do something about it.

Because your primary interest is student learning and because you are taking care and time to work on your exams, you are a different instructor from most of those your students will encounter. So your tests are different. What students have learned directly or indirectly from taking others' exams may not serve them well on your tests. Many of the test-taking tips loose in the general college student population work well on poorly constructed tests but not on well-constructed tests. One piece of advice is, when in doubt, choose B or C. This advice will work on poorly constructed tests because it relies on some item-writer psychology. Item-writers tend not to make A the key because they don't want the key to be first so that examinees need to read more of the options. They also tend not to put it last because it "sticks out". So they tend to "hide" the key in the middle, option B or C. Since you are randomly placing your keys, all options have a roughly equal chance of being the key. You probably should tell your students these kinds of things.

You can embed this test-taking preparation into your test-specific preparation by, for example, showing students what your items will look like, showing them directions, suggesting test-taking strategies.

Summary

A great many of the learning benefits to using MCQs actually occur before, and often well before, the test itself. Make sure you're maximizing those opportunities!

References and Resources for Further Reading

Bates, S. P., Galloway, R. K., Riise, J., and Homer, D. (2014). Assessing the quality of a student-generated question repository. *Physical Review Special Topics – Physics Education Research*, 10, 020105-1-11. http://dx.doi.org/10.1103/PhysRevSTPER.10.020105

Erbe, B. (2007). Reducing test anxiety while increasing learning: The cheat sheet. *College Teaching*, 55(3), 96–8. doi: 10.3200/CTCH.55.3.96-98

Fellenz, M. R. (2004). Using assessment to support higher level learning: The multiple choice item development assignment. *Assessment and Evaluation in Higher Education*, 29(6), 703–19.

Foos, P. W. (1989). Effects of student-written questions on student test performance. *Teaching Psychology*, 16(2), 77–8.

Kerkman, D. D., Kellison, K. L., Pinon, M. F., Schmidt, D., and Lewis, S. (1994). The Quiz Game: Writing and explaining questions improve quiz scores. *Teaching Psychology*, 21(2), 104–6.

12 How to Get Students to Think During a Test

One of the most frequent criticisms of multiple-choice questions (MCQs) is that they frequently require only memorization and cannot get to higher-order thinking, critical thinking, or the higher taxonomic levels. There are plenty of things you can do in order to have your MCQs reach those skills. We'll explore what you can do inside of the item itself, with add-ons, and with groupings of MCQs to get students to think during a test. We'll also look at some administration choices, like group tests.

You Always Have Options

Manipulating the options on a MCQ also manipulates the required cognition and likely the exact learning objective of the item. While it is true that MCQs always require recognition of the right answer, how challenging that recognition is can change. Consider this relatively rudimentary illustration from Olivia's history course. Imagine a stem asking when the Missouri Compromise was enacted. (Assume, for the moment, that a "date" question was important enough to include.) Were she to use this set of options: "a) 1790, b) 1800, c) 1810, d) 1820", with "d) 1820" as the key, it would be a purely chronological question. This set of options is also fairly wide and covers a broad and active span of US history. A student who has even a simplistic grasp of when slavery first became an active legislative issue, or who can associate it with Henry Clay instead of Aaron Burr as a legislator, could answer the question. A more discriminating but still chronological set of options would be "a) 1818, b) 1819, c) 1820, d) 1821". A final possibility is to move away from a purely chronological understanding to a somewhat more conceptual understanding by having the options represent years of significant slavery legislation: "a) 1794 (Slave Trade Act), b) 1820 (Missouri Compromise), c) 1850 (Clay's Compromise), d) 1854 (Kansas-Nebraska Act)". (Those parentheticals are there for your benefit; only the dates would appear on Olivia's MCQ.)

That example actually illustrates two different considerations: option homogeneity and option meaning. Option homogeneity refers to the degree to which the options are similar. The more similar the options are, the more discriminating students' knowledge and thinking needs to be. In Olivia's item, options differing by one year require better discrimination than options differing by 10 years. However, are the smaller differences meaningful or do they encourage memorization of facts and details? Option meaning refers to what the given options actually represent. Even though all three versions use dates, the third version uses the dates as proxies for events in the progression of slavery-related legislation. So that third version isn't actually a chronology question.

Process or Product?

Let's take Olivia's item one step further. When MCQs assess facts, products, or end results of reasoning, they are easier for students to address algorithmically or to guess. What if you focused on the processes, strategies, or concepts required to reach that product when constructing the MCQ? For a quick-and-dirty example, consider changing the source of options from outcomes (3 + 4 = 7 where 7 is an option) to processes (3 + 4 = 7 where + is an option). This fundamentally changes what thinking the scores represent. With Olivia's item, what if the stem remained the same ("When was the Missouri Compromise enacted?"), but the options now are these and not dates at all: "a) During the Constitutional Convention, b) At the beginning of the 'Senate's Golden Age', c) During the Nullification Crisis, d) At the outbreak of the Civil War"? While still a factual and somewhat chronological question, it now requires students to know where the Missouri Compromise fits into the larger fabric of the antebellum era; it's more conceptual.

Preet does this in her statistics course. Instead of asking "What's the answer?" formula questions, she asks conceptual and process questions about formulas (see Figure 12.1).

As you are writing items and you find yourself writing a "fact" question, see if you can recast the item to address *how* the student should be arriving at that fact. That's usually what you're actually aiming toward.

In the formula for a sample variance $\left(\hat{s}^2 = \dfrac{\sum \left(X_i - \bar{X}\right)^2}{(N-1)} \right)$, what is the portion which corrects the estimate for negative bias?

a) $(N-1)$**

b) $\sum$

c) $\left(X_i - \bar{X}\right)^2$

d) $\sum \left(X_i - \bar{X}\right)^2$

Figure 12.1 Example Process MCQ in Statistics

Add-Ons

One of the advantages of recasting MCQs toward process instead of product is that it is still accomplished inside the supplied-response item which can be machine scored. Another way to get at process, but which is more resource-intensive, is to ask students to explain their answer or to show their work to a MCQ. Doing so has many advantages. You can score their explanation, too. It illuminates what reasoning they're using to respond – information you could use to reteach, for example. It could also uncover item flaws, things you didn't realize would inappropriately distract students.

If you choose to have students show work or explain their choice and you want to score that, too, then you need to construct a scoring guide or rubric for their responses. Students need to know about that ahead of time, too.

Variations and Elaborations

In Chapter 3, we discussed mostly the mechanics of formats like the context-dependent item sets. One of the main reasons for employing context-dependent item sets and vignettes is to get different kinds of thinking from students. By using a more extensive stimulus material and asking questions about it, you can assess much more than recall. Providing the stimulus materials permits you to ask application, interpretation, and inference questions, and perhaps lots of them. There really is no limit on the size of stimulus materials other than time and logistics. Logistically it can help if students can have the stimulus alongside the exam rather than in the exam itself. Jay often makes stimulus materials the last page(s) of a paper exam and instructs students to tear that page off so it can be beside the exam itself. Preet can employ a second browser window for stimulus materials.

Figure 12.2 shows another example from one of Preet's exams. She asks 20 items set in the context of this one scenario; here, some of them refer directly to information in the stimulus.

Question 1 is almost a classic computation question, except that, with the stimulus material, the students need to know what to compute and where to find it in the stimulus. Also, Preet has written options which would reveal misunderstandings. In this situation, the investigator is employing an independent samples t-test, which has $(n-1) + (n-1)$ degrees of freedom, here $(20-1) + (20-1) = 38$ degrees of freedom. A student choosing 40 would be selecting the total sample size. A student choosing 39 would be demonstrating the naive understanding that df is always $n-1$.

Question 2 asks for a definitional element of a formula that isn't actually reported as such in the scenario. If the student knows that the numerator of Cohen's d is the absolute value of the mean difference, then she would have a couple of different places to look on the output to determine that value.

Scenario A

This example is modified from R. C. Sprinthall. (2003). *Basic Statistical Analysis* (7th ed.). Boston: Allyn & Bacon. It is on page 265.

Dr. Peterson is interested in whether there's a difference between scores on the Motivation for Continued Treatment subscale of the Maryland Addiction Questionnaire among inmates incarcerated for Operating a Vehicle Under the Influence. One group of 20 participants was assigned to a treatment facility for dealing with drug-abuse issues and the other group of 20 participants continued in the main jail with no treatment being provided.

Group Statistics

	Treatment	N	Mean	Std. Deviation	Std. Error Mean
Motivation for Continued Treatment Scores	Treatment Facility	20	48.0000	6.34118	1.41793
	Main Jail	20	41.0500	6.45205	1.44272

Independent Samples Test

		Levene's Test for Equality of Variances		t-test for Equality of Means						95% Confidence Interval of the Difference	
		F	Sig.	t	df	Sig. (2-tailed)	Mean Difference	Std. Error Difference		Lower	Upper
Motivation for Continued Treatment Scores	Equal variances assumed	.000	.983	3.436		.001	6.95000	2.02286		2.85493	11.04507
	Equal variances not assumed			3.436	37.989	.001	6.95000	2.02286		2.85489	11.04511

$$d = 1.08$$

Cohen's d is computed using the main jail group as the "control group" given the way the research question is worded above.

$$\hat{\omega}^2 = 0.213$$

1. What should the missing *df* value be for this *t* test?

   a) 40

   b) 39

   c) 38**

2. What is the numerator for the Cohen's d value reported?

   a) 3.436

   b) 41.05

   c) 6.95**

3. According to the output provided, do Dr. Peterson's data meet the assumption of homogeneity of variances?

   a) yes**

   b) no

4. Is there a statistically significant difference in the MCT mean scores for those inmates in a treatment facility versus those in a jail? Assume $\alpha = 0.05$.

   a) yes**

   b) no

Figure 12.2 Context-Dependent Item Set Stimulus Material and Related MCQs

Questions 3 and 4 are really application questions. Question 3 requires students to pull lots of different information together, including the skill of reading the output from the particular software used in the course (here, SPSS), in order to answer a yes or no question. It's actually a much more synthetic question than it appears to be.

Many aspects of context-dependent item sets were discussed in Chapter 3. We want to remind you here that the authenticity that can come with context-dependent item sets does change students' thinking during the exam. Putting even factual items into an authentic framework changes students' cognition.

The Group Test

Letting students work together during a test, either in pairs or groups, is a proven technique to change the way students think during the test. Wait! Don't skip this section if you're one of those who think "group test" is a non-starter. Hear us out on this for a moment. Yes, there are philosophical and validity objections to letting students work together, but there are also many benefits. Let's discuss some of the philosophy first and then do the cost-benefit analysis.

Philosophically, some instructors feel that a student's grade should reflect what that individual student knows, and should not be influenced by what other students do. We totally agree, but that doesn't rule out group-testing approaches. Most of the research on group testing shows that test scores are higher when students work together than when they take the test individually (e.g. Gaudet *et al.*, 2010; Stearns, 1996; Toppins, 1989; Zimbardo *et al.*, 2003). If you're a skeptic, you say, "No kidding!" But the relevant question is, did the scores go up because learning went up or for some other reason? Research done to distinguish the two have consistently shown that learning improves, which should be our goal. That is, the high grades in a collaborative condition do represent more and/or better learning. Some of the concern about whose grade it is also depends on the actual logistics. We'll discuss that in a moment.

Another reason to engage in group testing is one we've referred to before: because collaborating toward a group consequence is a professional skill. Two of the sources we read did an excellent job of arguing that collaboration on tests is professionally relevant: Toppins (1989) in human resources development and Sandahl (2009) in nursing.

There is definitely cost to enacting group testing but there are also benefits. The costs are usually incurred in doing group testing well. Group testing works well when students understand how to work effectively together in groups (Johnson and Johnson, 2004; Stearns, 1996; Toppins, 1989) and when you're using collaborative learning techniques elsewhere in your course (Hodges, 2004). It works well when you are testing higher-order content, not lower-order content (Hodges, 2004; Toppins, 1989). You also need to keep the test short enough to allow for discussion time (Toppins, 1989), which needs to be kept in mind when you're developing your test blueprint and writing items. Students also need to know ahead of time because group testing alters how students prepare, and the pairs or groups should study together and strategize about the test together prior to the test itself. Be aware also that some students will resist this strategy (Zimbardo *et al.*, 2003), so be prepared to articulate your reasoning for using it and to stick to your decision.

In terms of scoring, there are several variations in the literature. You can assign the group the average grade, or the grade of one group member can be chosen at random. However you choose to do the scoring, it is critical that you preserve one of the most important "active ingredients" of group testing: peer contingencies (Zimbardo *et al.*, 2003) or peer interdependence (Johnson and Johnson, 2004). Put plainly, the grade an individual will receive for the test must hinge on others' knowledge. Jenson, Johnson, and Johnson (2002) conducted a study in which some students had a group discussion and then recorded their own individual response about each test question, while other students' group discussion resulted in a single answer. The former group did not experience the benefits of group testing that the latter group did.

Another "active ingredient" is what the groups are discussing during their testing time. In addition to functioning well as a group, their discussion needs to be focused on justifications for each option (Stearns, 1996).

With those steps in place, you may see what others have seen: student test anxiety reduces before and during the test; student interaction before and during the exam is deeper and better; student interest in the subject and retention in the course is higher; and they learn more and better.

Having students work together during the test also provides you with insight into their thinking and into your instruction (Castor, 2004; Toppins, 1989). You can simply walk around and listen in during the test and learn a ton about what they know and don't know. You can also ask groups to construct justifications or explanations which you can review.

Using groups for assessment is a very complex topic, and we've just scratched the surface. For a short but more comprehensive treatment of this topic see Hodges (2004), and for a book-length treatment, which we think is phenomenal, see Johnson and Johnson (2004).

Summary

There are so many variations available to you during the test itself to promote higher-order thinking among your students. These kinds of possibilities make tests in and of themselves learning events that you and your students will value.

References and Resources for Further Reading

Castor, T. (2004). Making student thinking visible by examining discussion during group testing. *New Directions for Teaching and Learning*, 100, 95–9.

Gaudet, A. D., Ramer, L. M., Nakonechny, J., Cragg, J. J., and Ramer, M. S. (2010). Small-group learning in an upper-level university biology class enhances academic performance and student attitudes toward group work. *PLoS ONE*, 5(12), e15821. doi:10.1371/journal.pone.0015821

Hodges, L. C. (2004). Group exams in science courses. *New Directions for Teaching and Learning*, 100, 89–93.

Jensen, M., Johnson, D. W., and Johnson, R. T. (2002). Impact of positive interdependence during electronic quizzes on discourse and achievement. *Journal of Educational Research*, 95(3), 161–6.

Johnson, D. W. and Johnson, R. T. (2004). Structuring productive groups. In D. W. Johnson and R. T. Johnson, *Assessing Students in Groups: Promoting group responsibility and individual accountability*. Thousand Oaks, CA: Corwin Press.

Sandahl, S. S. (2009). Collaborative testing as a learning strategy in nursing education: A review of the literature. *Nursing Education Perspectives*, 30(3), 171–5.

Stearns, S. A. (1996). Collaborative exams as learning tools. *College Teaching*, 44(3), 111–12.

Toppins, A. D. (1989). Teaching by testing: A group consensus approach. *College Teaching*, 37(3), 96–9.

Zimbardo, P. G., Butler, L. D., and Wolfe, V. A. (2003). Cooperative college examinations: More gain, less pain when students share information and grades. *Journal of Experimental Education*, 70(4), 101–25.

13 After the Test

Just because your students have completed the test, this doesn't mean that the learning is over. There are a number of approaches for revisiting a test during which students can still learn and/or demonstrate mastery of learning objectives while also perhaps recovering part of their grade. The basic technique involves permitting students to revisit the test at some point after they've earned an initial score. The issues become, how long after? in what way(s)? and for what additional contribution to the grade?

Mastery Opportunity

Jay adapted a technique he learned from a colleague that she called the "mastery exercise". After students take a multiple-choice exam and scores are recorded, they receive their exams, copies of their answer sheet, and an answer key. They have a specified period of time during which they may write about each question they got incorrect. They are instructed to explain why the key is the best option, or to explain why their response is better than the key. For each item they missed about which they write correctly, they can earn half-credit. In order to earn the credit, their explanation must be correct; it cannot still contain any misconceptions; it must be substantive. Confession will not earn points (e.g. "I knew that C was the right answer but inexplicably bubbled D.").

This approach is useful not only for exams but also for lower-stakes assessments, like quizzes. Dawn employed a similar technique as a part of the team-based learning (TBL) system she used in her class. In TBL, students take an individual MCQ quiz on a reading assignment and then complete the same quiz as a team. Teams receive immediate feedback about the correctness of each MCQ and are allowed to submit a written "appeal" if they disagree with the correct answer to a question. Appeals must cite a reference source, in addition to providing an explanation as to why they think their answer is correct, and must be submitted immediately after the team quiz is completed. If their appeal is successful, teams receive full credit for the question.

This approach has many advantages as well as some drawbacks. Students tend to like this approach initially because it allows them to better their score. Then they report that they do, indeed, learn by revisiting the questions that they missed. Some report that they set out to prove that Jay and Dawn are wrong, and then, as they think and write about the items, they see the point and learn from the exercise.

Jay likes this approach because it diffuses some of the intensity around scores – students know they will have a second chance to better their scores. It also defuses any potential feeding frenzy (when "self-expression often trumps self-control" (Hampton, 2002, p. 62)) if exams are handed back en masse in class. You've seen that, we suspect; that dreaded period which Hampton (2002, p. 62) vividly captures: "Emotion supplants reason, the burden of proof shifts to the instructor, and venting compromises both learning and the search for fairness." Any questions from students about the exam are met with "do the mastery exercise, and if you still have questions, come to my office hours."

It also serves as a form of item analysis, revealing ways the distractors and items more generally are (mis)construed by students, and is the primary reason Dawn includes appeals in her TBL process. If the student explanations reveal an incorrect key or a second key (an option which is also correct), Jay rescores the entire exam for every student, not just those who found the error, giving any student responding to the second key credit. Fair is fair. Similarly, when there is an incorrect key, Dawn rescores the quizzes for individuals and teams. However, when there is a second option which a team successfully argues should be considered correct, Dawn only rescores the quizzes for teams that submitted a convincing appeal. She uses this approach to encourage teams to think through the options and provide cogent arguments for an answer that Dawn did not originally identify as the correct answer.

Jay's anecdotal sense is that the student understanding in the written responses is genuine. There's not much legalism and posturing. Dawn finds that her students write appeals when they often have a valid interpretation of an option that she had not considered. This helps her improve her questions for their next use.

Using this technique incurs costs in managing the logistics of getting exams and keys out to students, and collecting and scoring responses. Most problematic to some, it breaks test security and lets the exam and the key out.

Note that the way this is structured, it is not a grade giveaway. Learning must be evidenced in order for a grade to improve. By providing half-credits back per item, it still honors the original test performance, the original test preparation, the initial (mis)understandings, while still permitting additional learning not only to happen but to be rewarded with an increased grade. A student who initially earned a 70 percent can receive at most an 85 percent (30 percent missed/2 = 15 percent). While that is a change from a

C minus to a solid B, the increase is based on additional evidence of mastery of the material. It's not a curve or a points giveaway. So the resulting scores, we argue, remain valid as indicators of what the students know and can do.

Note also that, to emphasize fairness and learning, this opportunity is offered to all students regardless of score. The student who missed just one question, who thereby still has something to learn, can show mastery of that issue and receive half a question's worth of points, perhaps moving from a 98 percent to a 99 percent. To limit the opportunity only to certain students (say, those who earned less than a B), signals that the opportunity is about the grade, not about the mastery of the learning objectives.

Finally, this mastery opportunity is voluntary. If the 98 percent student wants to do it, he may. If the student who earned an 80 percent is willing to live what that, that's OK, too. The same is true when teams are allowed to appeal a question; teams may elect to appeal an incorrect question, depending on the collective desire of the group.

This technique is another one of our high-leverage activities because it achieves several different purposes. It emphasizes learning above, or at least level with, grades. It does provide a second chance to better a grade – if more learning is evidenced. It diffuses the emotional elements of getting scores back. It provides insight and information about what students are thinking and about your MCQs themselves.

Variations on the Mastery Opportunity

With that mastery opportunity as our point of reference, let's examine some ways to ring changes on it.

One way to address the security concern of letting students take the exams with them is to speed up the process described above so that it all happens within one testing session. Bloom (2009) describes spending approximately half of the testing time devoted to individual test-taking, individual answer sheets are handed in, and then a second answer sheet is provided. For the second half of the testing time, students may access notes or books, or, as another variant, students can work together either to produce a group answer sheet or individual ones; see Bloom (2009) for a full articulation of the logistics of this approach. He also presents evidence that students who do the second attempt collaboratively retain their knowledge more than those who do it individually.

Toma and Heady (1996) have a very similar approach they call "take-two testing". Similarly to Bloom, here students work for half the testing window individually and then work collaboratively for the second half. In take-two testing, the two scores are averaged. Toma and Heady report many of the same benefits as others we cite here do. This differs from the TBL approach Dawn uses in that the individual and team grades are not averages but rather are separate components of the student's overall course grade.

While these approaches provide some test security, it also reduces the "testing real estate", the amount of time, and hence the number of questions you can ask. So you'll need to weigh the costs and benefits of those choices for you and your students. There isn't a "right" answer.

Hampton (2002) uses a more generic grade appeals policy for any graded work. Jay's mastery opportunity adheres to many of Hampton's more general steps and rationales. In brief, students may write about any graded activity for which they did not receive full credit; they must be succinct, on point, and correct; they have one week to submit this.

The Graded Exam Activity

Williams et al. (2011) report on a required follow-up homework activity with its own point value called the "graded exam activity" in an Introductory Biology course. Here, MCQs from the exam that 40 percent or more of the students got incorrect are identified. Two of these are then given to students with the key, and their homework assignment is to answer the questions in Figure 13.1.

These questions are magnificent examples of our principle of leveraging existing activities. For Intro students, presumably newer to the college experience, question 1 is a simple way to goad them into a little metacognition about their learning. We discussed in a previous chapter whether or not it's our job to teach study strategies, and this is an excellent example of how low-cost, high-reward doing so can be. Questions 2 to 4 are great ways to have students reflect on test-taking skills. Williams and colleagues (2011) report learning gains on subsequent test performance and positive feedback about this approach from students.

Handing Back Exams Activity

Aldrich (2001) describes a method for handing back exams the class period following the exams. First, he emphasizes to students that their learning, and not their grade, is very important. Then students work in pre-existing groups to help one another understand why they missed the items they missed.

---

1. What lectures did the information come from?

2. Why is the right answer correct?

3. Why are the wrong answers incorrect?

4. Why did I answer the question incorrectly, or for students who answered correctly, why might my classmates have missed the question?

(Williams et al., 2011, p. 348)

Figure 13.1 Example Graded Exam Activity Homework Assignment

Their graded incentive for having these discussions is a five-item quiz drawn from the exam that will be given at the next class period, as well as a cumulative final that contains some of these same items.

This activity highlights two principles we've discussed elsewhere. First, the peers and not primarily the instructor become the source of feedback on student performance. Aldrich (2001) mentions that pitching these discussions to small groups, and hence to peers, and thus away from whole-class and from him as examiner, pushes the right answer from his to theirs. The ownership switches to their learning and away from his test. Nice! Second, it provides an explicit connection for the students between the feedback they'll receive now and the next assessment opportunity to which they can apply their learning. As we discussed earlier, feedback is more valuable to students when the next opportunity they have to employ their corrected knowledge explicitly exists.

Exam Wrappers

Lovett (2013) describes an approach, centered on study skills and exam preparation rather than on exam content, called the "exam wrapper". Wrappers are given to the students with their graded exams; students are asked to reflect on three questions: 1) How did the students prepare for the exam? 2) What kinds of errors did they make on the exam? 3) How should they study for the next one?

Why This Isn't Extra Credit

While the focus of this book does not permit us to make a full and formal review of the arguments for and against "extra credit", we do explicitly need to articulate here why the techniques in this chapter are not extra credit opportunities, and we really don't want you thinking about them in that way.

First, these opportunities are not extra credit because there is nothing "extra" about them: the credit has always been there for students to earn. There is no way for a student to receive a final exam score of more than 100 percent in the mastery opportunities, and, in the methods which add on another quiz or homework assignment, those carry their own value. They also tap student learning of the required learning objectives, so the content covered here isn't "extra" either.

Second, calling them extra credit instead of a "mastery opportunity" places the emphasis on grades, not on learning. The emphasis should be on additional learning, not on additional credit.

Summary

When the exam is over, the learning can continue! You'll need to work through the costs and benefits of these various options for you and your students, but don't miss one more opportunity to drive learning!

The End of the Beginning

In Chapter 1, we encouraged you to take a "deep seat and a far-off gaze"; that is, to settle in for a long, but ultimately profitable ride. You did, and we've covered a great deal of territory in this book. In many respects, though, your journey with enhancing your use of multiple-choice questions has really just started.

Hopefully, you've gathered some ideas about how you want to write questions differently; how you want to plan your tests; how you want to talk to your students about assessment; about how you want your instruction and their learning to change; about how you can spend a little time to save a lot of time and trouble. Perhaps you'll look into what technological choices you have on your campus for using MCQs in your instruction as well as on your assessments. Perhaps you'll talk to colleagues about what's truly important in your classes. We sincerely hope that this book has not only sparked lots of ideas for learning-oriented change but will also serve as a continual resource to you as you do that hard but rewarding work.

You've reached the end of this book, but your journey with MCQs for learning *and* assessment is just getting started. Winston Churchill, a true master of managing people's expectations, reminded the world as Allied troops experienced victory in North Africa in 1942: "Now this is not the end. It is not even the beginning of the end. But it is, perhaps, the end of the beginning."

We wish you and your students a magnificent journey!

References and Resources for Further Reading

Aldrich, H. E. (2001). How to hand exams back to your class. *College Teaching*, 49(3), 82. DOI: 10.1080/87567550109595853

Bloom, D. (2009). Collaborative test-taking: Benefits for learning and retention. *College Teaching*, 57(4), 216–20. DOI: 10.1080/87567550903218646

Hampton, D. R. (2002). Making complaining appealing. *College Teaching*, 50(2), 62. DOI: 10.1080/87567550209595876

Lovett, M. C. (2013). Make exams worth more than the grade: Using exam wrappers to promote metacognition. In M. Kaplan, N. Silver, D. LaVaque-Manty and Meizlish, D. (eds.) *Using Reflection and Metacognition to Improve Student Learning Across the Disciplines, Across the Academy*. Sterling, VA: Stylus Publishing.

Toma, A. G. and Heady, R. B. (1996). Take-two testing. *College Teaching*, 44(2), 61.

Williams, A. E., Aguilar-Roca, N. M., Tsai, M., Wong, M., Moravec Beaupré, M., and O'Dowd, D. K. (2011). Assessment of learning gains associated with independent exam analysis in introductory biology. *CBE – Life Sciences Education*, 10, 346–56. DOI: 10.1187/cbe.11-03-0025

Index